Separation Anxiety in Dogs

Next-Generation Treatment Protocols and Practices

Malena DeMartini-Price, CTC

Dogwise Publishing
Wenatchee, Washington U.S.A.

Separation Anxiety in Dogs
Next-Generation Treatment Protocols and Practices
Malena DeMartini-Price, CTC

Dogwise Publishing
A Division of Direct Book Service, Inc.
403 South Mission Street, Wenatchee, Washington 98801
1-509-663-9115, 1-800-776-2665
www.dogwisepublishing.com / info@dogwisepublishing.com

© 2020 Malena DeMartini-Price
Illustrations: Lili Chin
Graphic design: Lindsay Davisson
Cover design: Jesus Cordero

All rights reserved. No part of this book may be reproduced or transmitted in any form or by any means, electronic, digital or mechanical, including photocopying, recording or by any information storage or retrieval system without permission in writing from the publisher.

Limits of Liability and Disclaimer of Warranty:
The author and publisher shall not be liable in the event of incidental or consequential damages in connection with, or arising out of, the furnishing, performance, or use of the instructions and suggestions contained in this book.

Library of Congress Cataloging-in-Publication Data

Names: DeMartini-Price, Malena, 1968- author.
Title: Separation anxiety in dogs : next-generation treatment protocols and practices / Malena DeMartini-Price, CTC.
Description: Wenatchee, WA : Dogwise Publishing, [2020] | Includes bibliographical references and index. |
Identifiers: LCCN 2020037435 | ISBN 9781617812743 (paperback) | ISBN
   9781617812767 (ebook)
Subjects: LCSH: Dogs--Psychology. | Dogs--Behavior. | Separation anxiety.
Classification: LCC SF433 .D458 2020 | DDC 636.7--dc23
LC record available at https://lccn.loc.gov/2020037435

ISBN: 978-1-61781-274-3
Printed in the U.S.A.

Dedication

This book is dedicated to the most amazing group of dog professionals I know, the certified separation anxiety trainers (CSATs). Each and every one of them has become like family to me. It is such an honor to work with them. Our work with separation anxiety clients has grown tremendously as we increase in number, and as a result we have learned more and will continue to do so. This book is a culmination of the invaluable contributions of all of the brilliant CSATs. I thank them from the bottom of my heart for everything they have done and continue to do so.

Table of Contents

Acknowledgements

Thank you to all the people who helped tirelessly with this book. You are legion! First of all, to the team at Dogwise: You have been tremendous in your efforts to bring this book to fruition. Huge thanks to Larry Woodward for his steadfast guidance, Adrienne Hovey for her profound editing eye, both generous and detailed, and Jon Luke for being always supportive and kind. The wonderful layout was done by Lindsay Davisson, who is a treasure. Working with all of you is such a rewarding experience. Dr. Zazie Todd, thank you for your lovely foreword. You are a wealth of knowledge. Thank you to Eileen Anderson for her extraordinary editing assistance. It has impacted this book so positively that I don't have enough words of thanks to offer. In addition to your editing genius, I am so grateful to have been able to include the excerpt about noise sensitivity from you. The incredible artwork in this book was created by the ever-so-talented Lili Chin. I am grateful to work with her and to be able to use these impactful drawings.

CSATs Casey McGee, Lisa Waggoner, Tiffany Lovell, Tina Flores, Jane Wolfe, and Josh Boutelle, I send you my humblest gratitude. Your compelling stories, so generously written, are integral to the book. There is no better way to peer into the life of a guardian of a dog with separation anxiety, and how sweet the victory of recovery is. Dr. Amy Pike, I so appreciate your contribution from the point of view of a veterinary behaviorist. Having your perspective is priceless.

Thank you to Jean Donaldson, Kathy Sdao, and Ken Ramirez for your generosity in reviewing and endorsing the book. I know how much work that entails, and appreciate the time you contributed more than I can say. Lastly, thank you to my beloved husband, Kevin Price, for your diligent and patient support of me throughout the writing of this book. I could not have gotten through this without you and am grateful every day of my life to have your kindhearted care and encouragement.

Foreword
by Zazie Todd, PhD

Separation-related distress is a serious welfare issue for the dogs it affects, and very upsetting and difficult for the dogs' guardians. Being able to get reliable help for separation anxiety can literally be life-changing. Having spent years working exclusively with separation anxiety cases, Malena DeMartini knows all too well how tough it can be for people whose dogs are affected – but she also knows how to resolve the issue. I am thrilled that she has written this essential book that will make a tremendous difference to dogs' and people's lives.

The central tenet of her approach is that dogs should not be left alone for longer than they can handle. Although this may sound like a tall order, Malena explains why it is important, and has tips for how it can be achieved. Building a support village around the dog can enable dog guardians to maintain something of a normal life whilst keeping their dog happy. Meanwhile, the methodical plans outlined in this book provide a pathway to teach the dog to enjoy alone time. It really is "Mission Possible!" as she likes to call it.

Malena is nothing if not laser-focused on what the data is telling her. Because of that, many readers will find a few surprises in this book, such as not needing to leave food toys down for the dog. The reason is simply that she has found what works and what doesn't and, respectful of her client's time and resources, has eliminated the things that don't make a difference. But in addition to this measured, data-driven approach, Malena is full of compassion for the people who find themselves in the predicament of having a dog with separation anxiety. Whether it's busting myths, explaining the science, or describing training approaches, the text is clearly written and easy to follow.

The book includes helpful sections from other writers. Dr. Amy Pike discusses the potential use of psychoactive medication for dogs with separation anxiety. Eileen Anderson provides invaluable tips for sound-sensitive dogs, something that often seems to co-occur with separation anxiety. Casey McGee considers what shelters and rescues can do to help dogs in their care that have separation anxiety. And a set of case studies by Tiffany Lovell, Jane Wolfe, Tina Flores, Josh Boutelle, and Lisa Waggoner, as well as McGee and Malena, provide additional insights and an optimistic message to show that this approach really does work in the real world.

This book demystifies the process of helping dogs learn that alone time is not only possible but perfectly fine. I am excited that so many people will benefit from the wisdom in this book, and will be able to put in place plans to improve their dog's welfare and their own lives. Packed with expertise, this book is an invaluable resource for dog trainers who take separation anxiety cases.

Zazie Todd, PhD

Introduction

Why a New Book?

In 2014 I wrote *Treating Separation Anxiety in Dogs*. Much to my surprise and delight, the book sold very well and the reviews and feedback I have received have been positive. The success of the book inspired me to start the Separation Anxiety Certification Program for dog professionals, which has helped to propel a significant movement in the dog industry of furthering dog welfare for separation anxiety sufferers. Despite having worked almost exclusively on separation anxiety cases for 13 years before the publication of that book, I have something now that I didn't have then – data!

The new protocols I have created and honed with the help of the certified separation anxiety trainers (CSATs) are data-driven. We collect data on each individual case. We have hundreds of hours of video recordings of dogs during controlled, planned absences. Each of us reviews and takes data from recordings as a significant part of our workload. We keep spreadsheets that include lengths of absences, the individual dog's behaviors, and numerous observations about external triggers. And by combining and comparing our cases, we have aggregate data from which we can draw more meaningful conclusions.

Here's the thing: We have now learned even more about separation anxiety best practices together. The community of CSATs that now exists, and the data we share, allow us to both hone our general practices based on evidence and get informed help from each other on individual cases.

The last few years have also given us the benefit of more peer-reviewed research on separation anxiety. And the research shows that there has been improved efficacy resulting from the major modifications to our approach. This has also been externally confirmed in a peer-reviewed setting.

We have learned how to do this in the most direct, efficient, and compassionate way possible.

We now have a legion (100-plus strong at the time of publication) of CSATs around the world in many continents and time zones. While I am thrilled at having these trainers to help dog guardians, my personal reward has far surpassed that level of appreciation. I now have a team of like-minded people who excel at working with separation anxiety. I can rely on them to help further separation anxiety education industry-wide and push the limits toward continually advancing methods of treatment. These CSATs are like family to me and to each other. I'm no longer a lone soldier; I have a small army. It is an honor for me to see and learn from the growing skills of the CSATs as they have collectively and individually resolved so many cases.

So there will be some surprises in this new book for many people familiar with my earlier work. Many of the often-recommended components of separation anxiety training have shown themselves to be irrelevant to success, at times even detrimental. Suspend your disbelief, if you will, and let me show you what our data have revealed, and how our very high success rates reflect the changes we have made.

I understand that many people in the dog profession have relied on conventional treatment for separation anxiety, which, at its core, involves food toys, teaching behaviors, and the use of crates or confinement. This book will take a different direction that is a departure from some of those practices. While training operant behaviors and using positive tools like food toys and crates is incredibly valuable for some types of behavior modification, you will see that this is not the mainstay of what is suggested here. We have to remember that the essence of separation anxiety is fear and panic. The underlying panic is what has to be addressed, and accomplishing that is what is discussed here.

While I am delighted that my first book has provided a guideline for many trainers and dog guardians, I am so thrilled to create this current book, which I hope will blow open the doors about the nitty-gritty of treatment. There are practices we follow today that afford us enormous success with our clients, and I want to (need to) share all of it with you, my reader.

It is understandable that you may be looking for step-by-step instruction for training, sort of standard operating procedures, if you will. While there are definitely specific methodologies and principles that need to be implemented in order to achieve success with separation anxiety, I cannot provide detailed examples of the individual steps to take with a given dog. The essence of this training is, in fact, that you must adapt the training for each particular dog. There is no one size fits all, there is no exact duration exercise that will suit all dogs, and there is no automated or formulaic way to meet the needs of so many different individuals. We can, however, learn how to develop tailored protocols based on clear guidelines that address each dog's needs – understanding that process is the basis for the book.

While this book is intended for dog professionals, I include a discussion of guardian experiences because they are crucial to the process. The role that guardians play and the toll that it takes on them is tremendously significant. Throughout the book I will talk about having compassion and empathy for them and their dogs. Doing that, while following the processes outlined in this book, will help you set everyone up for success as you address this profound welfare issue in dogs.

I hope you find this guide useful and that you decide to work with separation anxiety clients at least in some capacity. They are desperately in need and genuinely willing and able to dedicate their time to their dog. Do know, however, that if you still find working with separation anxiety too overwhelming, there are lots of us out there who are more than willing to help! For those of you who find yourself excited about separation anxiety training through reading this book, I urge you to consider gaining further knowledge through the Separation Anxiety Certification Program. While this book is rich with information on treating separation anxiety, the education provided in the program is far more comprehensive.

The quintessential component to begin treating separation anxiety is not found in a food toy or by teaching a dog to perform a behavior.

The elemental factors required are compassion (for both the dog and his guardians), patience, and a carefully constructed plan. Their inclusion in a separation anxiety protocol will allow for both the dog and the client to live a fundamentally better life.

By focusing on the long game and having genuine concern for the dog's well-being, clients can be successful in their treatment of separation anxiety. This kindhearted path to successful separation anxiety resolution is the premise of this book.

By following the processes I describe, you will be well on your way to completely transforming the lives of dogs and the owners that love them so dearly.

What's included in this book

This book is going to explain the straightforward transformational process to address separation anxiety. I will walk you through the details of a separation anxiety protocol that is driven by humane principles, based on data, and that yields successful results. Despite the research available, separation anxiety treatment remains ambiguous in the industry. This book is intended to bring clarity to this frequently misunderstood issue.

Chapter 1 will focus on the nature of separation anxiety, what it is and what it isn't. We'll be reviewing some of the terminology associated with separation anxiety and briefly touching on related symptoms. Additionally, in this chapter is a review of the many myths and misunderstandings that surround this condition.

Chapter 2 covers the very important role effective management plays in the process. Additional discussion will include critical aspects to understand about effective training protocols. This chapter will also introduce the use of desensitization and the correlating concept of threshold. A grasp of each of those concepts is essential in order to proceed with implementing a proper behavior plan. The severity of separation anxiety is also discussed.

Chapter 3 reviews questions about the inclusion of feeding toys and confinement areas in separation anxiety protocols. The examination of those two components alone will hopefully give way to new insights into the treatment process. Additionally, there is a discussion on using food rewards with dogs during absence rehearsals, which is a common training suggestion.

Chapter 4 is about the substantial time and energy commitment required for both the trainer and the dog guardian to treat separation anxiety. Learning how to work effectively with both the dog and the human during separation anxiety training is so important that it merits its own chapter. This chapter will review the various "must haves" for trainers and for guardians. This chapter will include discussion about reading body language, using technology, the business of treating separation anxiety, and some brief review of learning principles. Furthermore, this chapter will talk about some of the intangible requirements for both trainers and guardians, including a few scripts that help.

Chapter 5 approaches the nitty-gritty of treatment. Here, we'll focus on implementing behavior plans, a process that involves both the trainer and the dog guardian. In the behavior plan segment, we will walk through everything from the initial assessment to the actual day-to-day training process, which will also include some discussion on tracking data, technology use, regressions, and pre-departure cue incorporation. All of the particulars of an efficient and effective separation anxiety protocol are laid out carefully to guide you.

Chapter 6 includes a section on medication and alternative remedies as these may provide the best supportive treatment for many SA cases. There is some discussion here about working with veterinarians, and a special section written by a prominent veterinary behaviorist is also included.

Chapter 7 includes recommendations for diverse situations such as puppies, noise phobia, multidog households, and separation anxiety dogs in shelter/rescue. While these topics are separated, they are no less important.

Chapter 8 includes case studies and stories that will serve as examples of some of the principles in the book. There is one written by me, in addition to others written by trainers who have completed the Separation Anxiety Certification Program, which illustrate real-life experiences.

You will also notice that I have cited many of the important research studies published over the past couple decades for those of you who want to review this valuable information further. The full bibliographic information is included in the References section in the back of the book, listed alphabetically by author last name.

Two quick notes

There are a few words and bits of grammar I would like to point out before you delve too deeply into your reading. As is common in many books about dog training, I was faced with the decision of using "he" or "she" when referring to dogs. (Interestingly, many sources still say to use "it," but I just couldn't bring myself to call my beloved friends "it.") I have chosen the male pronoun in my writing based on a coin toss. My own dog is a female, but the coin came up heads, so there it is. When it reads better, I also sometimes use singular "they" or "them." Please know that, of course, what I write applies to dogs of both sexes and humans of all genders.

This book is written for dog professionals who are working with separation anxiety clients; however, I have tried to avoid jargon when possible so that dog owners can follow along and oversee their separation anxiety protocol if desired. I also have developed an online self-paced separation anxiety course specifically for guardians called Mission: POSSIBLE, for those who prefer to learn that way. The course can be found on my website: malenademartini.com.

Chapter 1
What Is Separation Anxiety?

Those of you who have owned dogs all your life or trained them for your profession will have likely come across at least a few dogs who were suffering with separation anxiety. It is a tremendously common issue, and considerable research on the topic has been published in the last 40 years. The research routinely proclaims the pervasiveness of this problem. According to work by Flannigan and Dodman published in the *Journal of the American Veterinary Medical Association*, separation anxiety is "one of the most common canine behavior problems" (2001).

In a 2020 study by Luciana de Assis and colleagues called "Developing Diagnostic Frameworks in Veterinary Behavioral Medicine: Disambiguating Separation Related Problems in Dogs," the following statement was made: "Between 22.3–55% of the general dog population are believed to show these signs, and they make up between 14 and 40% of dog behavior referral cases."

Separation anxiety is a welfare issue for dogs in that they are not only suffering, they are at risk of losing their homes, being returned to a shelter or even euthanized. In the New Zealand publication *Veterinary Medicine: Research and Reports*, Rebecca Sargisson states "Indeed, separation-related problem behaviors are commonly cited reasons for relinquishing dogs to animal shelters" (2014).

Separation anxiety is born of a natural evolutionary mechanism that is present in all social animals (humans included). Separation anxiety exists to protect young or naive individuals from the real dangers of being left alone or moving too far away from an environment that provides protection, and thereby being placed in a perilous situation. It is a heritable trait that serves a specific function and improves a social animal's fitness or survival. When a condition exists for such reasons, which is also known as its having adaptive significance, it is essential to recognize it as such.

Separation anxiety, therefore, should be recognized as having an evolutionary function. A young canine who suddenly finds himself drifting away from his family unit cries out and makes it easier for his parents to find him. (Independence from the parents only appears when the animal is biologically and psychologically ready for it, and comes gradually.) This is not unlike the reaction a puppy may have when left alone for the first time.

One study notes that "Fear and anxiety are among the most fundamental emotions required to survive or cope in potentially dangerous or harmful situations … A fundamental emotion, such as fear, may, however, turn into pathological traits when prolonged and generalized." (Tiira et al., 2016) This means that fear, in and of itself, is a normal part of life. Because of this, I personally do not refer to separation anxiety as a disorder, aberration, or illness in most cases. The research literature is explicit about the clinical nature of separation anxiety and often refers to it as pathology. I understand the use of that terminology for the scientists. For the layperson, however, I think there is significant reason to avoid language that implies such a significant deviation from being normal or healthy. After so many years of working with separation anxiety dogs and their guardians and having a separation anxiety dog myself (now recovered), I am sensitive to the feelings that surround the dog's condition. The more profoundly we lean into language that implies grossly maladaptive or pathological behavior, the more often I see clients begin to give up or think that their dog cannot learn to be alone. Labels can in and of themselves be harmful.

Confusing terminology

Separation anxiety is a clinically diagnosed condition that needs to be carefully defined, compared, and contrasted to other problem behaviors. There are numerous concerning alone-time behaviors that are not actually separation anxiety, although they can appear similar to the untrained eye. Some examples are alarm barking, housetraining mishaps, and other behaviors born of under-stimulation and lack of enrichment. If those behaviors appear without the presence of anxiety, a different training protocol may be required.

Sherman and Mills (2008) note that terminology used can add to the confusion: "There is overlap between the definition and common use of the terms anxiety, fear and phobia, although the underlying neural and emotional systems may be different." It bears mentioning here that there are separate and individual definitions of anxiety, fear, and phobia when used in research or in the medical community. Ballantyne (2008) defines each of these as follows: "Anxieties, fears, and phobias refer to emotional, behavioral, and physiologic responses to threatening stimuli. Although these terms are sometimes used interchangeably, they refer to different emotional states and may have different neurobiological mechanisms." Ballantyne differentiates the terms like this:

- "Anxiety is anticipation of a danger or threat. The stimulus for the response is not always identifiable or present."
- "Fear is an emotional, behavioral, and physiologic response to a stimulus that the animal perceives is threatening."
- "Phobia is a persistent and maladaptive fear that is out of proportion to the situation or stimulus."

Many dog professionals can generally identify when a dog is experiencing separation anxiety versus other concerning alone-time behaviors. It is nonetheless vital that we review what separation anxiety is, to ensure that we are correctly identifying this condition.

As a side note, I will refer to this alone-time condition as separation anxiety in this book. However, the more common presentation is actually isolation distress. The clinical condition of separation anxiety is when a dog does not tolerate being alone without his specific person or people; in other words, only Mom or Dad's presence is sufficient for the dog to not experience distress. With isolation distress, any person accompanying the dog will do; it does not have to be the main caregiver. There is a fair amount of muddle in the terminology surrounding alone-time anxiety, even within the research literature. Frank Cannas and colleagues (2014) state the following about the use of the varying terminology: "Undesirable behavior problems that occur during owner absence are published under various expressions, such as separation anxiety, separation-related problems, isolation anxiety, separation reactions, separation-related distress, and separation anxiety syndrome."

Further discussion about the identification of alone-time behavior issues is found in a publication by de Assis and colleagues (2020). They state: "Although these cases are relatively easy to identify, there is some debate over the different forms of the problem, and these cases may be variously described as having 'separation anxiety,' 'separation related disorders' or 'separation related problems.' There is also undoubtedly inconsistency in the use of this terminology since there is no 'diagnostic' test that defines a specific underlying biological mechanism."

Separation anxiety is an anxiety condition

I don't think it is a surprise to you to hear that separation anxiety is an anxiety condition – my goodness, it has the word "anxiety" in the name, so it's pretty clear, right? However, it's not as clear as one would expect, and the severity of the issue is often overlooked. These dogs are experiencing veritable panic when they are left alone, and it is behaviorally critical. A behavioral emergency (or behavioral crisis) occurs when the sufferer of a condition experiences episodes of fear and anxiety. This emergency can overwhelm them and result in further detriment emotionally or physically. We see many separation anxiety sufferers degrade in their condition when not treated. Sherman and Mills (2008) state that: "Treatment is often delayed until problematic responses are extreme, such as occurs with panic reactions or reactions to multiple stimuli. Animals with these problems may be perfectly normal at other times and may not be described temperamentally as fearful."

I personally consider virtually every genuine case of separation anxiety or isolation distress to be severe. Even those dogs who are not destroying the house or jumping out of windows still warrant the commitment to comprehensive training – they are suffering. We'll be digging in a bit more about the severity of separation anxiety in Chapter 2.

Separation anxiety is also a very common problem behavior, and unfortunately often results in an untreated dog being handed over to a shelter. Recall from this book's introduction that research by Flannigan and Dodman showed that separation anxiety is among the most common canine behavior problems, diagnosed in 20 to 40% of dogs that are referred to behavior practices in North America. Blackwell et al. (2006) state that "When behavioural problems are given as a reason for handing dogs into rescue centers, it is estimated that 33 percent of them are related to separation; these problems are therefore a significant, although largely unrecognised, welfare problem for dogs in the UK."

There are no quick fixes

In her article on the progress made in understanding separation anxiety in dogs, Ogata (2016) states: "In the past four decades separation anxiety has been the most commonly discussed disorder in published studies of experimental research and retrospective research in the fields of applied animal behavior and veterinary behavior." I feel strongly that the prevalence of separation anxiety discussions in the literature is *a very good thing*. It means there is a lot of scholarly work to turn to when treating it. However, she does go on to say,

"Etiology, treatment, and prevention remain elusive." This statement is often mirrored in the beliefs of humans whose dogs experience separation anxiety; the one thing that virtually no client can even fathom is that separation anxiety is fixable. While it's true that there are no quick tips or tricks to resolve separation anxiety, the potential for resolution is excellent when a proper behavior modification protocol is followed.

Surprisingly, the knowledge that there are no quick fixes has been around for a long time, even though it is not reflected sufficiently in a typical internet search. In 1982, Victoria Voith and Peter Borchelt released a study called "Diagnosis and Treatment of Separation-Related Behavior Problems." Referring to separation anxiety, they stated in their article: "There are no single and simple panaceas for these (or any other) behavior problems." (Voith and Borchelt, 1982)

I know that a magic wand for separation anxiety would be lovely, and we all daydream about its existence. There is no magic wand. Instead of the quick fix that we are wishing for, we must understand the incremental process of working with separation anxiety. It's slow, it's challenging in many ways, but it is effective. And trainers who learn and understand this process can convey that to their potential clients who are suffering along with their dogs. Trainers can offer hope and can impart their own confidence in the process. Later in the book you'll read a story about a dog named Holly. She was a pivotal case for me. Working with Holly brought me to the strong belief that we can be successful with this process with time and consistent training. I'll remind you on several occasions that separation anxiety is fixable so that you can come to the same strong belief that I have.

It is a challenging process

I am well aware that working with separation anxiety is challenging; I have lived it personally and professionally for two decades. I would never guarantee behavior outcomes, but I can offer you one promise. The process in this book has helped an inestimable number of dogs and those who love them, which demonstrates that separation anxiety resolution is indeed possible. A thorough understanding of the process, including an appreciation for the need for compassion, will serve you and your clients well as the experiences of our clients have shown.

This book has been written with every ounce of my soul included. There is nothing that brings me more passion than seeing both clients and dogs thrive during (and after) their separation anxiety training, and I poured all that I have into writing on their behalf.

Separation anxiety myths

Before getting too far into the nuanced areas of separation anxiety management and training, it will be helpful to dispel the many myths about treating separation anxiety. Many trainers, unfortunately, subscribe to some of the myths, but the bigger challenge is likely having to dispel myths for your human clients as part of your efforts to get them to commit to the behavior plan you choose to adopt. This is a general list of the most common myths, but there are many more that I have not included. Think carefully about what is being said or suggested before considering a change in how you work with separation anxiety.

MYTH: The client caused her dog's separation anxiety. This is not the case. It is often said that she let the dog sleep in her bed, she carried him too often, she petted him too much, she coddled his fears, and was even told she rewarded his anxiety. These things do not cause separation anxiety.

MYTH: Separation anxiety is not treatable. Like any fear, phobia, or anxiety issue, there are favorable treatments that can make a difference and lead to a reduction or complete resolution of separation anxiety. The reality is that we need to use the appropriate methods and be aware that they are not quick fixes. Whenever I hear someone say, "I tried everything, and nothing worked," I question their definition of "everything."

MYTH: Medications are a last resort. Waiting until everything is collapsing, and the client has used every last mental and financial resource, is not the right time to consider medication. Separation anxiety is a welfare problem for the dog and, in many ways, for the guardian, too. Please don't wait to explore meds as an option. We'll talk further about medications to make sure you are aware of accurate, useful information about the options, and I encourage you to be open to the possibility for a separation anxiety dog.

MYTH: The dog is behaving out of spite. Dogs don't have this sort of cognitive ability in their repertoire, so we don't even need to entertain this discussion. See the discussion below in this chapter on guilt for more information.

MYTH: Only rescue dogs get separation anxiety. We have worked with dogs from excellent breeders and even very young puppies that experience separation anxiety. We are now seeing studies that show that genetics likely plays a role in separation anxiety, so don't believe the myth that it is only dogs with "bad" experiences or rescue dogs who have separation anxiety (Bradshaw et al., 2002).

MYTH: Some breeds are more likely to experience separation anxiety. Considerable information discussing breed-specific characteristics exists, and some breeds are labeled as being prone to separation anxiety. While I suspect that there will be more information as further genetic studies are revealed about separation anxiety, at this point it appears that separation anxiety is not a breed-specific issue. Sherman and Mills (2008) discuss the fact that no specific breed category seems to be overrepresented consistently with regard to separation anxiety. They do, however, mention that mixed-breed dogs show a higher prevalence in the research, but it is important to remember that the relative percentages of purebred dogs versus mixed-breed dogs who are diagnosed with separation anxiety vary from study to study. Their overall deduction was that no bias was observed when compared with the representation in the general population.

MYTH: Dogs "grow out" of separation anxiety. Forgive me if this is glib, but do you outgrow your heart disease, diabetes, or depression so very easily? As a clinical disorder, your dog will also not likely outgrow separation anxiety. Additionally, if you expect to let your dog grow out of separation anxiety while leaving him alone regularly, you can exacerbate the problem or at best leave the dog to suffer for a long while needlessly (Wright and Nesselrote, 1987; McCrave, 1991).

MYTH: The dog can be left alone sometimes when working on separation anxiety training. This is incorrect. When we are working through a separation anxiety protocol, the dog must experience no stressful absences. Other than the times the client is doing specified training, the dog will not be left unsupervised. Any absences outside of training that would cause undue stress have the potential to cause considerable setbacks to the critical work being done when working on separation anxiety.

MYTH: Getting more exercise will cure separation anxiety. Exercise is excellent for all dogs, but being exhausted from a good run or jaunt in the park is not what will fix separation anxiety. The more exercise a person gets for their dog, the more of an athlete they will create (and the more of an athlete they create, the more activity their dog will potentially require). I am not advocating for *less* exercise than the dog gets currently, I'm merely pointing out that exercise is not the "cure" for separation anxiety. (Note: Exercise can be highly beneficial in the resolution of other behavior issues such as boredom or under-stimulation.)

MYTH: Getting another dog will fix separation anxiety. Several research papers (Lund and Jorgensen, 1999; Parthasarathy and Crowell-Davis, 2006; Ballantyne, 2018) suggest that most dogs with separation anxiety are not helped by getting another animal (be it a dog, cat, fish, or gerbil). For a very small handful, an animal companion helps, but the underlying anxiety still exists when the buddy is not present, so this is truly just a Band-Aid and is not recommended as a fix.

MYTH: Many dogs with separation anxiety will need to be euthanized. Absolutely not. As a behavior issue that has a good track record of being resolved, separation anxiety leads to euthanasia only in very rare and unusual cases (typically when medical complications are also at play). I want to be very transparent here that our goal is always to keep the dog's welfare in mind. For dogs who are genuinely suffering and cannot find a suitable home (as sometimes happens in rescue situations), euthanizing may, unfortunately, be the most humane option in some cases.

MYTH: Clients are reinforcing bids for attention by re-entering the home if their dog is vocalizing. The dog is vocalizing because he is anxious, not because he is trying to call someone back. You cannot reinforce anxiety behaviors like this. If I hug you while you are anxious about an upcoming exam, will that "reinforce" your anxiety? Please tell me your answer was no. If your dog barks at you for a treat, you can absolutely reinforce that, but reinforcing deliberate behavior (like barking at you for that treat or jumping on you for attention) is vastly different than the incorrect notion of being able to reinforce an emotion. Separation anxiety is an actual panic issue. If a dog has been diagnosed with separation anxiety and barks while the client is out, this is a result of panic, so it may be more illuminating to think of the barking as the outward sign of an internal state (panic), rather than a straightforward voluntary behavior. The client need not worry that she is reinforcing barking in the traditional sense of the definition. Having said all of this, you will always be striving to have the client return when the dog is not vocalizing or displaying anxious behaviors, as that is the basis of remaining under threshold.

MYTH: Dogs with separation anxiety must be crated. This is a ubiquitous suggestion. While occasional dogs with separation anxiety can do well with crating (particularly those who are already completely in love with their crates), most dogs with separation anxiety do much better without. Confinement anxiety is an extraordinarily frequent issue with separation anxiety dogs, so assessing whether the dog can do better outside of the crate is particularly important. See Chapter 3 for more information on this topic.

MYTH: If the dog is left with a food toy, he'll have something to do and not be worried about the fact that his guardian is gone. Some dogs won't even eat when left alone, but those who will eat usually display anxiety the moment the food is gone. See Chapter 3 for more information on this topic.

MYTH: Leave your dog with a T-shirt, blanket, or sock that smells like you. Hang on! Your whole house smells like you, so this really won't make a difference for actual separation anxiety! (Why does this one always make me snigger a bit?) Yes, you have likely seen online posts about leaving your clothes wrapped onto a mannequin to "trick" your dog into thinking you are there via scent and sight. If these dogs were genuinely experiencing separation anxiety, this would not work, and at the end of the day, I urge you to never "lie to your dog" anyway.

Never lie to your dog

So many proposed ways of changing dogs' behavior consist of trying to distract them or lie to them. Our intentions are usually good. Step-by-step training can take time, but if someone claims there is quick fix, it's human nature to want to try it. We could argue that there is a moral issue involved with lying to our dogs (and I believe there is), but there's a more immediate reason not to do it. It doesn't work.

Dogs' noses are superb; they know the difference between the odor on a T-shirt you wore yesterday and living, breathing you. Same with a mannequin – you have flesh and blood, not stuffing. And you breathe. When you leave the TV or radio tuned to a talk show to try to convince a dog that there is someone in the house with them, do you think, with their excellent hearing, that they buy that for one minute? When you talk to them through a digital device, but they can't smell or see your body in a normal way, is that the same as your actually being there? Even leaving mounds of food toys in the hopes of distracting a dog long enough is a form of lying. We are trying to convince them not to notice that we are gone. But they notice.

Never lie to your dog. It doesn't work.

MYTH: Training will boost a dog's confidence, so engage in lots of activities that will make a dog feel more secure overall to fix separation anxiety. There is no correlation between the training of other types of behaviors and improvement in separation anxiety symptoms. Having said that, please know that it is terrific to train dogs for all sorts of reasons, and you can encourage your clients to do so. I just want you to know that things like obedience training, agility, or nose work, while excellent, are not instruments to fix a dog's separation anxiety. Additionally, separation anxiety training can be time-consuming, so asking a client to engage in tons of other training activities that won't have much (if any) impact is not a recommended practice (Voith et al., 1992; Flannigan and Dodman, 2001).

MYTH: Leave the TV or radio on to keep the dog "company." While we sometimes recommend background noise like a radio or white noise machine, these are typically suggested to protect against potential upset due to external sounds that we can't control. (An example would be apartment building noises that the dog is sensitive to.) Separation anxiety is commonly comorbid with noise phobia, so this sort of intervention can help mitigate fear-provoking sounds for those that are affected. Sounds for keeping the dog company are not necessary. If sounds are used to protect from extraneous noise, this should be done systematically, and the sounds should be chosen carefully in order to carry no risk of scaring the dog themselves. See Chapter 7 for more information on noise phobia and usage of sounds.

MYTH: The owner must be their dog's pack leader. This advice is outdated and not accurate. Dogs are not out to take over the world or assert dominance over us. Not only is this advice outdated and factually incorrect, but it is also harmful – especially when it comes to things like separation anxiety. Dogs deserve our understanding, and as our loving companions, we owe it to them to recognize their needs.

MYTH: If the dog isn't punished for his alone-time destructive activity or urinating, he will not know it is wrong. Research from Borchelt and Voith (1982) indicates that punishment can increase a dog's emotional dependency on his owner. O'Farrell (1986) noted that punishment contributes to a dog's general anxiety level. Punishing dogs who suffer from separation anxiety is not only counterproductive but cruel. Imagine being yelled at for your fear of flying during take-off, or slapped for your fear of driving over a bridge *while* driving over the bridge! Those things would not only be awful; they'd be heartless. Please remember this if your personal frustration starts to mount. Take a deep breath and remember that your dog is experiencing panic, fear, anxiety, and stress. He is not a bad dog; he is scared out of his mind.

MYTH: Training a Velcro dog to not follow is the key to treating separation anxiety. If you think that addressing clinginess in dogs is the key to separation anxiety, you may be surprised to hear that it is not (Herron et al., 2014). A dog who follows his or her owner a great deal is not necessarily a dog with separation anxiety. We have seen numerous examples of confirmed separation anxiety dogs who were initially called clingy and remained devoted owner followers even after the separation anxiety was completely resolved. Persistent owner following is not necessarily a result of anxiety. Many dogs just like to be with their people a lot, and that doesn't have to be looked at as an abnormal attribute. To further confirm this, I'd like you to look at the graphic in Chapter 4 showing the percentage of dogs who follow their owner closely is high in both separation anxiety dogs and non-separation anxiety dogs.

Some myths are worth exploring in more depth due to the concerning subtext that correlates with their existence. Often times people consider that separation anxiety dogs are simply being naughty or are spoiled, and both of these descriptions need to be dissected.

The myth of the naughty dog

I feel people must understand that separation anxiety-related behaviors are emphatically not indicative of a dog being naughty. There is no malicious intent on the dog's part, nor is there a speck of revenge-seeking, despite what is commonly discussed amongst the general public.

Calculated reasoning is not in a dog's repertoire.

The guilty look that some dogs display is commonly used as a case argument for the naughty-dog-syndrome. However, it has been shown in many studies that these guilty-appearing behaviors are born of something completely different. The appearance of guilt is typically associated with a fear response to the owner's reaction.

Guilt is not a dog-construct, as *dogs have no moral compass.* (I remember hearing that sort of statement initially from Jean Donaldson, and it shook me to the core. If it does the same to you, please know I relate.) Many people disagree with that statement, but I would urge you to consider this or research it further while thinking critically. Being virtuous requires a type of cognitive reasoning that dogs do not possess.

Helpful definitions

Moral compass: An internalized set of values and objectives that guide a person with regard to ethical behavior and decision-making.

Virtuous: Conforming to moral and ethical principles; morally excellent; upright.

Dogs can react to our irritated or angry emotions, even in the absence of punishment. One example that I found fascinating was a study I read years ago (sorry, I can't remember the author to give a reference). If a dog defecates in the house, and the client gets angry (maybe just sighs, yells, or worse), the dog can become fearful. If the dog has a history (however brief) of Mom getting angry at alone-time indoor elimination, he can begin to exhibit a look that may be interpreted as guilt. This look is simply born of association and is anticipatory in nature.

Interestingly the study elaborates that if one were to take feces from the yard and place it in the middle of the living room (even an unfamiliar dog's feces, by the way), the dog can still show signs of fear or appeasement. It is, therefore, not the act of defecating in the house that the dog is "regretting" or showing remorse over, but rather the association of the presence of dog feces indoors when the owner arrives home after an absence. This reaction in itself is fascinating, but let it ring true for all of us that the guilty look is not a sign of compunction.

The statement "he knows better" needs to be removed from our dog-related language!

The myth of the spoiled dog

I'd like to open this section by asking if you (personally) spoil your dog.

The percentage of you, my dear readers, who talk to their dogs in a baby voice or as if they are human, let them sleep on the bed or couch, give them lots of treats and in general love on their dog in multiple ways, is high! (By the way, if you aren't doing at least a few of those things with your dog, you not only have my permission to do so but also have my encouragement in most all cases.) If spoiling a dog through treats, sleeping arrangements, snuggles, and cuddles were a *cause* of separation anxiety in dogs, the percentage of dogs with this condition would unquestionably be far higher than the currently reported figures. This is supported by McCrave's study (1991) in which it was found that there was no significant difference between the two groups (SA and non-SA) in how owners interacted with their dogs.

If you are saying "phew" to yourself, I'm so glad! If you are still wondering if you are causing your dog's separation anxiety, please carefully read on.

I have worked with countless numbers of separation anxiety dogs since 2001, and I gave each client permission to continue to show those dogs the affection they desired. This includes sleeping in bed with them and other practices that are often deemed as spoiling habits.

When you read the suggestion that a client should remove affection from their dog, please reconsider following such advice. Not only is excluding love-giving behavior not effective in reducing or eliminating separation anxiety, but it can also increase a dog's anxiety, as they are deprived of such affection, particularly if they have become accustomed to it already. Yes, this statement is potentially going to be debated by some professionals, and I welcome that. I hope that you use your personal critical thinking abilities to make your own decision about the accuracy of this declaration.

Extensive studies in children show that an environment where they are deprived of physical and emotional kindness and affection can lead to detrimental results, such as having poor social, coping, and problem-solving skills. When a child receives compassion and love, they are far better equipped to be a well-balanced and confident individual. It appears to be no different with our dogs.

Please remember that bestowing generous amounts of love on your dog is different than being behaviorally indulgent or permissive. Dogs (like children) do need to be taught about the general house rules, but that does not require the absence of kindheartedness or the inclusion of punishment.

When clients contact us for help with their dog's separation anxiety, it is entirely too common to witness them blaming themselves for their dog's issue. I spend a lot of time listening to tears and hearing people's heartbreak over criticizing statements they have heeded from people who were likely well-intentioned.

But separation anxiety is seldom a result of a client's mismanagement. Every owner of a separation anxiety dog must be told that the problem they are facing is not their fault. This lack of blame should be very clearly understood, and all guilt should be absolved. It should be hash-tagged and painted on billboards. If nothing else comes from the teachings in the book, I hope that this notion is understood and widely shared by trainers, veterinarians, and dog guardians.

Quite frankly, even if clients *were* somehow blameworthy, what good would it do to dwell on that and impose condemnation anyway? We should be focusing on implementing a positive plan for resolving the separation anxiety moving forward.

The process of including patience and compassion through gradual training has been successful for client upon client. Elements of our training plans are specifically designed to help the clients on their journey. You may be wondering why this compassion is so critical. It is with this compassion that clients can maintain patience through the gradual and often challenging separation anxiety training.

To give a little further evidence about the lack of owner liability in separation anxiety cases, I'd like to touch on the genetics of separation anxiety. There has been mounting research in the past years that indicates separation anxiety may likely have a genetic component. I have reviewed several studies that discuss separation anxiety genetic linkages, including an identified haplotype (Rooy et al., 2016; Mervis et al., 2012). As a non-geneticist, reading the research was challenging for me, but the gist of the findings is exciting. Do recognize, though, that while the potential heritability is profound help from the standpoint of removing owner blame, it does not mean that separation anxiety is any less treatable.

Chapter 2
Suspending Absences

I went into detail in my previous book about managing a dog with separation anxiety so that he never has to be alone longer than he can handle. I am happy to do so again because this is such a crucial component for successful separation anxiety resolution. This great quote from Sherman and Mills (2008) illuminates the role of management: "The purpose of environmental management is to reduce manifestation of signs and reduce strain in the household to permit time for behavior modification and pharmacotherapy to become effective." My experience shows that management is the most critical element to treat this problem.

No alone time

I am a strong proponent of suspending absences, i.e., not leaving the dog alone, as a crucial part of treating separation anxiety. I know this is a bit controversial, so before I continue, I would like to give a nod to all the trainers, vets, behaviorists, and dog owners who disagree about the need to manage a separation anxiety dog's alone time. I honestly appreciate your concerns and empathize with the challenges of implementing a management strategy – I really do. I would like to respond to that concern a bit.

I feel so strongly about suspending absences because it allows the process to move efficiently toward resolution while also keeping the dog from additional undue distress. Recurrent stress is no small thing; it is a health and welfare issue in addition to the fact that it tremendously hinders progress. I believe management is doable, and our data support my belief.

Of the last 2,000 prospective clients who filled out a contact form for Malena DeMartini Inc., just under 50% were already not leaving their dog alone, and an additional 30+% replied that they could suspend absences if needed. To clarify, that is upwards of 80% of people with separation anxiety dogs who were either already not leaving their dog alone or were willing and able to make that happen. The other approximately 20% who said this was not something that they could do often changed their minds once we explained the reason behind the necessity. Let's also not forget that the 2,000 inquiries I am referring to here were from many different parts of the world and represented a vast range of socioeconomic status.

Suspending absences can be done and is being done all the time. Not doing this for your dog is a dealbreaker for me. If you are training a dog for whom being alone is scary even for short periods of time, then you cannot suddenly leave the dog alone for longer periods of time. This will arouse fear and anxiety. It will almost always go wrong in one way or another.

I hope you realize through reading this book that what we are asking of clients through management comprises the most efficient, effective, and expedient way to get to the point of resolution.

Suzanne Hetts (2012) makes a strong statement in this regard: "Regardless of the type of fear, it is well documented in the learning literature that continued exposure to the fear-producing event significantly interferes with the successfulness of these techniques."

There are other ways to approach working with separation anxiety that some prefer to support, which take a lot longer and have a far lower success rate, but I feel that it is my ethical obligation to offer that which is going to be best for both owner and dog.

Efficiency is a priority in all training, but in particular in separation anxiety training. Because the separation anxiety training process can take a long time and be taxing on emotions and finances, the quickest means to resolution is essential. Following a well-organized and competent protocol is one way to ensure that the client can hang on through the finish line.

Why suspend absences?

Let's look at an example outside of separation anxiety.

Let's say that as a trainer, you are working with a dog who displays fear-aggression toward children. You speak to the client about all aspects of their training plan. Maybe you request that the dog be trained to wear a muzzle, that he remain at a specific (significant) distance away from children, and that the client use desensitization and counter-conditioning for their protocol. The client will also need to learn some leash skills such as a turn-and-go when they are faced with children approaching too quickly. This client is committed, and they tell you that they are on board with your plan except for one small variance. Every Tuesday afternoon, they hold a children's reading group in their home, and about a dozen kids are milling about. They say that they don't have any dog sitters to use, and there is no way they can restrict the dog's access to the children in the home during this time.

Wait…what?

I presume that we can all agree there are many concerning elements with this digression from the plan, not least of which is the potential for injury. In addition to the immediate threat of a bite, can you see that you would be damaging the training plan every time the dog was put into this overwhelming situation? I can't imagine any training professional would agree to move forward like this, because management would be so critical to avoid disintegration of the progress made (if any).

Here's the rub.

Why are we willing to be especially adamant about management in this training scenario but not with separation anxiety? Is it merely because we think the risk is higher? In part, I suspect we are sensitive about inconveniencing the client, yet having a dog with separation anxiety is one of the most significant inconveniences of all, so let's be truthful there.

If you still think separation anxiety management is impossible, don't toss this book in the bin just yet; please hang in there a bit longer.

Frequently, dog professionals tell the client that it would be "in their best interest" or "preferable" not to leave the dog alone, but this is fundamentally giving the client permission to do so, or at least giving them an option. It should be a requirement for the client to uphold this management practice during your training, so let's not ask if they would be willing to. Let's tell them that they must, but also explain carefully "why" it is obligatory and how to accomplish it.

Is that a difficult request? Yes, it can be.

Create a contract with the dog

When speaking with clients about management, I like to use the example of creating a contract. There are many ways you can convey the importance of management; this is just the one that I use personally. (I encourage you to come up with your own explanatory illustration, and I would love for you to share it with us too!)

We want to create a contract with the dog about alone time. We shake the dog's paw (metaphorically) and solemnly swear to only leave the dog alone during specified training. Furthermore, that training will always take place using a duration that the dog is comfortable with. That is the client's piece of the contract.

Fortunately, there are two sides to this contract. The dog is "making a promise" as well. Because the dog will be staying within his comfort level (threshold), he can agree not to vocalize, destroy things, or eliminate in the home.

Sometimes the beginning duration for training is a mere few seconds, but that's fine because we can build on that in increments to eventually become several hours. And no, it will not take 10 years to accomplish success, even if we are moving along in tiny increments. As we progress through the protocol, things will start to accelerate so we can add more substantial chunks of time to the absence. (Think about compounding interest growth as a model of how duration will increase.)

Progress Over Time

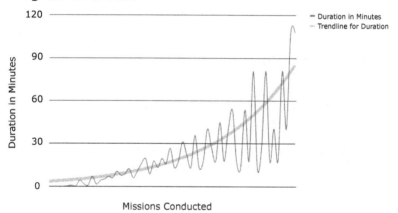

In the above graph that shows separation anxiety progress over time, you'll see that there is an upward trendline. This trendline (called an exponential trendline) is important for us to see, since we want to be certain that our progress over time is moving in a positive direction. The trendline is rarely very steep in separation anxiety training, but it is steady. You may wonder why there are so many large fluctuations in the chart. If so, you are a smart cookie to be questioning it! You will learn about this later in the book, but we intentionally create easy wins for the dog in order to gain further strides in our improvement. Mixing up the difficulty of the duration over time should still yield a positive trendline.

An applicable example:

We've been training with Fluffy and her guardian, Sally, and have worked up to a 45-minute duration of comfortable alone time. An old college pal calls and says he is blowing through town today and would love to get a cup of coffee to catch up with Sally. The coffee shop is 20 minutes from home, meaning there will be only a few minutes for chatting if she were to stick to the acquired duration (20 minutes there, 20 minutes back and 5 minutes of chatting). Sally decides just to go anyway and to make it a quick one. Twenty minutes later, Sally meets up with the friend, and they get to reminiscing. Time passes, then she suddenly realizes that she really must get home. By the time Sally is on her way home, more than hour has passed, meaning that it will be about a 90-minute absence in total.

Meanwhile, at home, Fluffy dozes a bit at first and watches the birds outside the window. At 30 minutes or so of alone time, Fluffy starts to get a little more restless, but she knows this "game" from her training, so she is all right until 45 minutes have passed. After that, more minutes pass and Fluffy (being keen to her training duration) starts to get a bit antsy. Fluffy eventually starts to whine mildly and begins a little pacing around. By the one-hour mark, she is showing some signs of anxiety. By the time that Sally arrives home, Fluffy has already gone into a full-blown panic just as she used to – howling, pacing, and drooling.

Our first reaction to this poignant scenario may be that we feel terrible that Fluffy was upset and anxious. Unfortunately, that is not the only troubling aspect of having stayed out too long. *We broke our contract.*

That one break of the contract has effects that go beyond those terrible minutes for Fluffy. It will be no surprise if tomorrow, when we begin our training absence, Fluffy will not settle successfully from the get-go.

The safe training that had been keeping Fluffy from experiencing anxiety has had a rule change, and it is understandable if she is now wary early on in an absence again. Trust me, unraveling all the hard work that goes into a training plan like this is the very last thing we want to do. This is why it is so important to uphold the contract through to the finish line. We can actually make the dog worse (sensitization) if we continue to leave them alone on occasion for longer than they are ready for.

What in the world can be done to help Sally and Fluffy to uphold the contract? First of all, as mentioned above, helping Sally understand why management is so essential is fundamental in getting a commitment. Doing a thorough job of setting the rules and expectations of a separation anxiety protocol with the client is something we categorically must do. Read on for other ways to avoid alone time.

Using outside resources to avoid alone time

Beyond getting that commitment, I feel that the main limitation to managing Fluffy's alone time is lack of creativity. There are many resources for people who need to not leave their dog alone, and upholding this contract is very doable. To reiterate, many of our clients are already managing absences (or most absences) when they contact us. When we speak to them about creating this contract with their dog, there is rarely any objection once they understand why this is so important. The roadblock is usually how to execute it.

There's good news here. The resources out there for support are abundant. As trainers, we can help our clients consider a wider variety of alternatives.

Daycares, dog sitters, and dog walkers

Many people automatically assume that a doggy daycare will be necessary, but while that option is fine if the dog enjoys it and if the cost is doable for the client, it is not the right solution for every case.

Having someone come to the home to care for the dog can be a better option for many, and this is not as difficult as it may seem. Think outside the box. What group of people can help create a village of dog-caretakers? The most obvious choice is friends and family. Their willingness to help is often a given, and they tend to charge little or nothing to do so. I know that not everyone is fortunate enough to have friends or family with flexible schedules nearby, but plenty of additional options exist.

We sometimes need to look outside our immediate circle for people who have flexibility. People who work from home, people who are retired, college students, or even mature teenagers are all options. All that is required in most cases is that the dog is not left without company. I will add this caveat here because, for a small subset of dogs, the separation anxiety is such that they have to be with their "person," and no one else will do. This is known as clinical separation anxiety, versus the more common presentation of isolation distress, where the dog is comfortable as long as someone (typically anyone) is present. Finding flexibly scheduled people can be a little work, but friends, family, and coworkers are usually able to spread the word, and neighborhoods often have plenty of people willing to help someone in their community.

We can also look into engaging an all-day dog walker or even a partial-day dog walker if we only need a few hours during the day. This can be great for people who will eventually need the dog walker to break up the dog's day during longer periods of alone time. The dog will start to learn early on that fun stuff happens when the walker arrives and that nothing terrible happens when the dog walker leaves. Schedules can be coordinated so that longer and longer absences occur before or after the dog walker has come, and this is an excellent way to extend training.

There are loads of great sites available to allow clients to reach out to people through social media. One of the favorites that we have here in the U.S. is called Nextdoor.com. This clever social media platform allows members of specific neighborhoods to sign up for an online group. Anything can be discussed in the group, from garage sales and potluck dinners to, yup, dog sitting! If your neighborhood has yet to start a Nextdoor.com group, you can do it yourself; it's enjoyable and beneficial for the neighborhood community overall. (I know this personally, as my husband started one in my little neighborhood.)

Family and friends

Let's not forget that our friends have friends whom we don't personally know who might be willing to help. Doing a mass email to all of our friends or posting a compelling request on Facebook can yield lots of resources to fill the village. (Accompany those requests with a heart-melting photo of the dog, and people won't be able to resist!) In some cities, there are websites specifically devoted to people who want to care for dogs. A fabulous example of this in the U.K. is called BorrowMyDoggy.com. There are various similar sites in other areas of the world that are worth exploring.

A note of caution: Individuals who are not trusted personal friends or family should be thoroughly vetted. While there are heaps of resources out there, I urge caution in selecting completely unfamiliar individuals. Additionally, have a document available for anyone who is caring for the dog that details everything: the closest vet location, the food and medication the dog consumes, and any quirks that might be important. (Examples: He is uncomfortable around large dogs, or he is not good off leash.)

If tapping into all of the above resources doesn't yield enough coverage, keep looking, and stay creative! There are pet sitters who could help, although they are typically more expensive than the other options. There are lots of retirement groups out there that are set up to help people find "work," and many members would be thrilled to spend a few hours or a day with a furry friend. Some work environments are very dog-friendly, so even if your client doesn't work in a dog-friendly office, a friend or colleague might. One example of getting creative is from one of our CSATs. The client she was embarking on working with had just moved to the area and had no friends or family there. After some failed attempts to find dog coverage, they decided to create a compelling flyer about the dog and his management needs. They asked the drivers at Meals on Wheels to distribute them. Not only did she find some dog sitters to help, but she also ended up having to create an online signup calendar because there were so many people that wanted to watch her dog. Creative solutions like this are endless.

And please do emphasize to your client that management is not permanent. You will be training the dog so that, in time, the absences he can handle will become longer and longer, and the people who are helping can do less and less.

Chapter 3
Food Rewards, Interactive Toys, and Confinement Areas: Pros and Cons

There are two tools of the trade that have long been a mainstay of separation anxiety training: interactive feeding toys and confinement areas, including crates, baby gates, and pens. Below I've outlined my feelings on the use of these tools, which have evolved as I learn more about what purpose they serve and whether they actually enhance the training protocol. In addition, this chapter will explore the use of food rewards during a separation anxiety treatment protocol.

Interactive feeding toys

For so many years, I read literature that instructed me that the key to separation anxiety training was food toys or other long-lasting food-chew items. So I used interactive feeding toys with all of my client dogs and got them to build up to expert-level noshing. Frozen Kongs, bully sticks, marrow bones, and treat balls of all sorts were mainstays in my early days of SA training.

Years into my practice, I started noticing something that gave me pause. The dogs who didn't eat when left alone (termed "alone-time-anorexia") were progressing at a tremendous rate, sometimes significantly faster than the dogs who were chomping away for a while during an absence. Interesting, right? I started to rethink my methodology.

I'd like to preface the remainder of this section with a clear disclaimer. In my experience of training dogs for all manner of behavior issues since 2001, I have come to see that the use of food in training is unquestionably the most efficient and effective means of reward. (Yes, some dogs prefer their ball or other toys, but distilled down, most will work diligently for food.) As a positive reinforcement trainer, I always have and will continue to shout from the mountaintops that food is truly the best means for achieving proficient dog training. Now, read on.

There are excellent reasons to use feeding toys with dogs, and we will talk about those, but the one place where I not only think they are unnecessary but can be a hindrance is in the early stages of separation anxiety training – surprised to hear me say this? Many are.

When feeding toys make sense

Let's first look at all the reasons why and when we should be using interactive feeding toys. An ideal time to use the best of the best of food toys is if the client is introducing a confinement area. Confinement areas are not actually necessary for most separation anxiety dogs, but we will discuss them in detail later for the dogs who need them. In the meantime, know that if one is needed for some reason, we should make that confinement space a veritable Disneyland for the dog up front so that he learns to love it. Confinement is covered in more detail later in this chapter.

The other way I like to use feeding toys such as the Tricky Treat Ball or similar types of toys from the Kong Company is to teach dogs to choose distance away from their guardians. Some dogs tend to be glued to Mom or Dad and will not ever walk too far away. We can help build some comfort with distance when using interactive feeding toys like those mentioned. Lots of dogs will stop eating their dinner if the caretaker walks away; that is how much they dislike being alone.

The toys I have mentioned here (and there are others like them) are suited to help with this if it is of concern. These toys roll around and dispense a meal or treats. The dog is in control of how far they are willing to be separated from the guardian. If the toy rolls too far from the owner for the dog's comfort, he can pick it up and bring it back to the original location nearby. Many dogs go absolutely wild for these toys and, in time, start to choose to let them roll farther and farther away, even out of sight into another room. When using these toys, the dog is the one choosing the distance to suit his comfort level, rather than the trainer or client dictating the space by teaching a stay and walking away. Nifty, right? Using such a toy for feeding or treat time is not a requirement for treatment. I like to add this for some dogs whom it might help, particularly if the client enjoys this sort of activity as well. These toys are only to be used when the client is home and is not intending to leave anytime soon. Do not use feeding toys during alone-time training, at least not initially.

When not to use feeding toys

What about using food toys during the actual separation anxiety desensitization plan? There are many problems that can arise when we use feeding toys or other food items in our protocol, and some research suggests they may not help at all (Herron et al., 2014).

The first concern about using feeding toys during our absence training time is that we will get a very false read on the actual absence. Many dogs will eat when left alone, yet the moment the toy or bone is done, they start to panic. Can we really expect the dog can tolerate a 20-minute absence if he finishes his toy at 20 minutes and begins howling at 21? Actually, no – this is simply a distraction for the dog, potentially a powerful one, but a distraction nonetheless. I would call that a one-minute (or less) absence where the dog could be without a feeding toy and still not be displaying external anxiety signs. This non-organic read of alone time can be confusing and tricky to work with. We cannot definitively determine that the dog is comfortable just because he is eating food at the beginning of an absence. A chewing dog may appear content or quiet, but eating is not in-and-of-itself sufficient to support the assumption of the dog's comfort, particularly when anxiety indicators pop up the moment the food is gone.

I'll leave you with this: I know that I can personally cry into my bowl of ice cream (mint chip for me) and feel anxious through to the very last spoonful. What about you? What about your dog?

One of the other concerning details about using food is that it can become a crutch for the human as well. If you have a dog who is initially distracted with 20 minutes of food-toy time, the client will think that they have a successful 20-minute absence. As a result, they may push the envelope on that because the dog is seemingly content. When we start to push the dog past his anxiety point after the feeding toy is done, there are several dangers. One is turning the toy into an adverse departure cue. Look closely at how this can happen, because it is a widespread occurrence when using feeding toys in separation anxiety training.

Mom gives a food toy and leaves. Dog eats food toy and finishes. Mom is still gone, and the dog becomes anxious. Eventually, food toy = absence, which in turn becomes food toy = anxiety. After enough repetition, the food toy becomes a reliable, tangible predictor that the absence will be too long. In time, the dog may begin to appear anxious when the food toy is presented. This is often referred to as poisoning a departure cue.

I once had a seminar participant tell me what happened to her SA dog when she was using feeding toys. At first, her dog was content with a toy stuffed with some wet food and kibble. After a while, the dog became leery just at the sight of that toy. In her efforts to combat the problem, she graduated to a different feeding toy and stuffed it with high-value treats. In time, the same concerning anxious behavior ensued when the dog was presented with the new higher-value toy. With understandably good intent, she made her way up the food hierarchy as the dog systematically stopped eating various food toys unless one was presented that was a higher value than the last. Eventually, she was giving raw marrow bones, and for a time, the dog was presumably content. As you are probably imagining, yes, even the marrow bone ultimately became a cue that the absences were too long. Unfortunately for this dog, he started to associate "all things food-related" with the potential of a scary absence. The client was ultimately reduced to sitting on the floor, hand-feeding the dog as her only option for getting food in him. That is a sad tale for sure, and I find it pretty staggering that the fear and anxiety surrounding being left alone could turn a dog off eating altogether. Not all dogs will reach such an extreme, but I hope the example gives you pause.

Because you are a dog professional and savvy with all things training, I suspect you may be considering one of two things: Wouldn't it work if we gave the feeding toy at other times of the day as well? Or what about if we always return while the dog is still eating (or just finished eating). Good for you for supposing this and using your critical thinking cap!

Giving the feeding toy at other times outside of the absence is a smart thing to consider. Unfortunately for us (good for them), dogs are masters of discrimination. Giving a feeding toy when you are wearing your bunny slippers and PJs while watching TV is quite different than being ready to go out (keys in hand, etc.) and giving it then. Dogs will and most often do discriminate the difference.

Furthermore, if you choose always to come back while the dog is eating or just finishing eating, you are faced with two problems. The first is how long will it take to complete the toy "today"? The second is, well, now what do we do to get more alone-time duration than the feeding toy can provide?

Don't worry, though. Feeding toys are brilliant, and if you do want the dog to have them during an absence, you can introduce them later in the protocol when the dog is no longer experiencing as much anxiety about alone time.

There are a few remaining reasons that food is not ideal when working in the early stages of a separation anxiety protocol. As an example, I mentioned that I could easily eat my bowl of ice cream while being thoroughly upset, anxious, and even crying. Many of these dogs are just so hardwired to eat food that they wouldn't leave it, but it doesn't mean that they aren't experiencing anxiety *while* consuming it. The fear escalates the moment the food is gone. I have a video of a dog who is eating a filled Kong and whining at the same time. She is pretty fixated on the food, but her conflicting motivation for experiencing anxiety while also eating is apparent. While some dogs may not display this conflict so overtly, I suspect such conflict exists in more dogs than we realize.

For many of you, the dogs you have worked with will not eat at all regardless of the value of the food left behind. It's a moot point for those dogs, but I mention it here because it plainly shows the tremendous impact that anxiety can have.

Should you reward the dog for tolerating an absence?

You might have read that the way to get the dog conditioned to successful alone time is by leaving for a short duration (seconds even) and then giving a treat upon return. When using this method, it is indicated that the treat is supposed to act as a reward for the dog "not displaying anxiety." This practice can certainly appear as though it is working for a while, but there are some very important considerations to contemplate.

Think about whether it is possible to *reward* a dog for the *absence of an emotion.*

Now that you've had a think on that, I'll tell you straight up: You can't reward an emotion, much less the absence of one.

When you give a treat on return, you are most likely rewarding whatever the last thing was that the dog did. Most often, you are rewarding the dog for approaching the door when you re-enter. Understandably, that is not what you want to be doing. Remember that you can reward behaviors, not emotions, so you must look at the *physical behavior* that is being rewarded in this scenario.

When using this approach, you are turning alone-time training into what's called an operant *contingency.* The keyword here is contingency, meaning the dog does X behavior, and a reward follows (the treat is contingent on the behavior). In this setup, the goal is that the dog learns that lying down without movement means a food reward will follow. As I pointed out, in a real-life absence, the dog will most likely get rewarded for getting up and meeting you at the door. But even if you succeeded in teaching a dog to lie down the whole time you were gone, and you reinforced that with food, you cannot reward a *feeling of calm*. You've just put a contingency on the *behavior of a dog who is scared*. And teaching duration behaviors (such as a down-stay) can be challenging even in the absence of anxiety.

As a side note, I can't help but think that if I were having a panic attack (as these dogs are effectively having), telling me to lie down would result in one thing only – panicking while lying down instead of while standing. The other concern here is that the goal of this type of training tends to be "maintaining a reclined position." We often say in our CSAT group that expecting "suspended animation" with a home-alone dog is not our objective at all. Dogs should be free to stand, stretch, walk around, sniff, drink some water, or just gaze out the window.

This method might look as if it is working for one minute or even several minutes because the dog will potentially remain lying down in exchange for the treat. But, at some point, that little piece of cheese or chicken is weighed against a far-too-expensive behavior. Would the dog still "work" for his treat after 15 minutes of lying down, or an hour, or an afternoon?

I certainly appreciate that this manner of training can give the impression that it is working in the beginning, and that can make owners feel enthusiastic. Actually, for some dogs who are not experiencing separation anxiety, but rather just acclimating to a new home environment, this process might not flop altogether. Dogs with actual anxiety about being left alone, however, will likely not be able to learn to successfully be alone with this treat-upon-return method. It will typically backfire as duration increases. The client will think it is effective for a while and feel optimistic, but when the time alone becomes too expensive for the dog, the training crashes, and they will have to start over with a different process. They may as well start with the more effective instruction from the get-go, wouldn't you say?

The final concern here is that we are actually bringing *more* attention to the guardian's return if we implement training in this manner. The dog is understandably fixated on their upcoming reward, which can mean that they won't relax at all. I think of what happens when I start actively training my dog – she is psyched and fully engaged.

This is not what we want from a dog who should be chilling out when left alone.

Confinement: yes or no?

The use of a crate or other confinement area is a standard public recommendation for separation anxiety dogs. In my first book, I reviewed at length how to use a baby-gated area. However, I can now state with confidence that *confinement is not necessary for treating a separation anxiety dog and can sometimes exacerbate the problem.* In fact, confinement anxiety often goes hand in hand with separation anxiety, so we have to be exceedingly careful to assess whether confining the dog is going to be prudent or helpful.

The most common reason people feel they should confine the dog is if the dog has displayed destructive behavior or elimination issues when left alone, but let's take a look at this reasoning. As long as we are working a protocol where we are staying beneath or at the dog's threshold, we won't run into a situation where destruction or stress-related elimination occurs. If teaching the dog to be confined in an area of the home is causing training challenges, one should definitely consider letting the dog be generally free in the house. Of course, bedroom and bathroom doors can be closed off, but many dogs do better when they have some openness. Note that I say "many" dogs, which I suspect is really "most," but there are always exceptions with sentient beings.

Some clients initially insist that confinement is necessary. When assessing a dog whose owner is determined to use confinement, I recommend that you use video. Record the dog once in confinement and once when free in the house. Make sure that you do these assessments separately, preferably a day or more apart. The bit of anxiety from the first assessment may produce a false read on the second assessment if they are done too close together.

I suggest setting up the camera in a place the dog is likely to go, which is usually the exit door. Having an angle that allows you to view the dog's facial expression is best. Sometimes you will see subtle signs that the anxiety is starting, such as a drawn mouth or a little bit of panting, so keep that in mind when setting up the camera angle if possible. (Don't worry, you can't always get the camera angle right the first time, and that's really OK.)

If the dog's reaction when free in the house is better than when confined, I don't even suggest trying to spend time getting them used to the confinement for separation anxiety training – just go straight for allowing the dog to be free in the house. (I am definitely an advocate of getting a dog comfortable with crating/confinement for other reasons like vet visits, car rides, etc., but home-alone-time is not one of them.)

And yes, I do realize that if the dog is considerably less anxious when free in the house, you may still have a tricky discussion ahead of you with a client who remains adamant about confinement. Remind the client that you will be keeping the dog under threshold during your training and therefore destruction and anxious elimination will not be occurring. Additionally, if the client is still really stuck on confinement, you can strike a small bargain with them. I let clients know that I will remain open to using confinement, but for the coming week or so I'd like to proceed with the training while the dog is free in the house. I agree that, if the dog becomes destructive or potties in the house during our training, I will be happy to discuss going back to using confinement.

In all my years of training this way, I have not once had to return the dog to a confinement area. Not once.

Chapter 4
Separation Anxiety
Treatment Basics

As a trainer, there is a long list of skills and knowledge you should possess before taking on separation anxiety cases and working hand in hand with human clients.

These include:

- Understanding the pros and cons of labeling the severity of separation anxiety.
- An awareness that separation anxiety is like a panic attack.
- An ability to express empathy toward your clients.
- Willingness to support your clients throughout the process.
- Mastery of the terminology related to separation anxiety.
- Facility using technology to observe dogs alone.
- Ability to track your data.
- The necessary time and availability to support your clients.
- The confidence to proceed, including:
    - An ability to read dog body language.
    - Knowledge of training methods.
- An understanding of how to desensitize dogs to being alone.

Severity of separation anxiety

As alluded to above, I want to talk a little about labeling the severity of a dog's separation anxiety. This labeling is something I've come to feel strongly about in the past years. I formerly classified a dog's anxiety as mild, moderate, or severe. While there is some merit in grouping like that for us as professionals, I think categorizing the dog's anxiety level can be harmful in many ways.

Imagine being afraid of spiders. (I don't have to pretend on this one at all!) When you see a spider, you start to scream. That is the way you react to the offending arachnid. Carol, on the other hand, sees a spider and, in her fear and panic starts to hurl objects at the spider. When Susan sees a spider, she begins to weep quietly, walks into another room, closes the door, and texts her partner saying that she will not emerge until the spider is gone. As you can see, we have three different reactions to spiders.

Which person would you say is the most afraid of spiders? Who is experiencing the highest level of fear and anxiety? Is it you?

Can you say that Carol is more afraid of spiders than you are? Can we determine the severity level of the anxiety based on the outward manifestation? I don't think so, which seems tricky, I know.

You can see where I am going with this. If Fluffy vocalizes when left alone, Rover destroys doors, and Charlie poops everywhere, are we able to discern which of those three dogs is most anxious?

The intensity of the outward behavior does not indisputably represent the severity of the anxiety. Fear and anxiety are internal states, and the level of suffering is not always equal to the outward manifestation.

When I do public presentations, I often ask the audience to raise their hands if they will take on mild separation anxiety cases. A good percentage of dog professionals will raise their hands, which is fantastic. When I proceed to ask if those same people would consider taking on a moderate or even severe case of separation anxiety, most of the hands quickly withdraw. Lots of dog professionals are apprehensive about working with those cases, and I fully empathize with such concerns. There hasn't been sufficiently recognized widespread education about how to work with separation anxiety, so the understanding of how to systematically progress with a training protocol is, at best, murky for many.

When it comes to severity, though, there is excellent news: The severity of the dog's display of symptoms is not a significant indicator of the ease or difficulty of the resolution. A difficult-appearing case may not necessarily be hard or lengthy.

Dogs who appear mild in their expression can take just as long, if not longer, than dogs who display more severely. More simply stated, dogs with severe-looking symptoms don't always take longer to resolve than mild. We are often worried about the severe form of a dog's symptoms and thus fret about the difficulty of the outcome, yet the dog will proceed expeditiously when a proper training protocol is performed.

I recently graduated a dog whose symptoms were not particularly dire looking, but it took two years to get to the point that the dog could successfully handle alone time. Conversely, there are so many dogs I have worked with who were extreme in their anxiety display, but they were better in a handful of months. (More on time frames later. Don't stress out about it now, please!)

No two separation anxiety cases are exactly alike. There are different particulars that must be incorporated into each individual's protocol; however, the basic principles for addressing separation anxiety are the same. Please read that statement carefully, as I do not want anyone to think that there is a one-size-fits-all training plan.

It is the principles that remain unchanged in a protocol, not the execution of those principles.

Now that you understand that the appearance of severity is not a discriminating factor, you may either be reticent to take on any separation anxiety cases or, conversely, be excited to take on all of them. Both of those reactions are thoroughly appropriate. Just be honest with yourself. Is separation anxiety a good fit for your training skills and personal temperament? If not, refer separation anxiety clients to another trainer (find a CSAT!). Plenty of dogs with other issues need your help.

Most clients who contact us say that their dog has extremely severe separation anxiety, and I surely don't want you or anyone to somehow minimize what they or their dog is experiencing; there is no need to disaffirm them. (The video assessment you do with the client is the information you need, as opposed to relying on their perception of the issue.) There are many aspects of client counseling that require thoughtful language, and this is one of them. In fact, I feel that whatever case is currently in front of me is the urgent one; they are all serious.

Timeframes: setting expectations

The most common question we hear from clients who are considering starting a separation anxiety protocol is this:

How long will it take?

I recommend that you have more than one answer prepared for this question, and none of them should include a specified timeframe. Remember, there are no guarantees in behavior, and we currently have no crystal ball. (If you do happen to have one, by the way, please sell it to me!)

The closest I ever come to offering a timeline for treatment is to tell the client to "think in terms of months, not weeks." Having planned, confident responses to the above question will serve you well. Also, remember: Always be transparent and do your best to set realistic expectations with your client.

Separation anxiety is a like a panic attack

Separation anxiety is akin to a panic attack. The stimulus (alone time) is what the dog is afraid of, and that fear can be surprisingly extreme. I realize that many clients don't understand why the dog is experiencing this panic, since they have always returned home after the dog has been left alone. Unfortunately, fears, phobias, and anxiety are not always logical to the outsider.

Perceived threats are just as significant to the individual as real threats.

Even humans with superior cognitive function experience seemingly irrational fears. A good example can be seen in the percentage of the population that is afraid of flying. Nearly a third of Americans are either anxious about flying or afraid to fly, according to flyfright. com. While we all understand that this fear is common, would we agree that it is rational? According to Dr. Arnold Barnett of MIT, "A person would have to fly on average once a day every day for 22,000 years before they would die in a U.S. commercial airplane accident." This pervasive fear of flying is rarely assuaged by quoting this figure or other statistics from the National Transportation Safety Board. Fear of public speaking, spiders, heights, and more have the same irrational properties.

Looking at other phobia types helps us see that always coming back home after an absence is not necessarily enough to relieve a phobic dog. (There is also the genuine issue that, with dogs, we can't merely "explain" that we will always return. If we gained the ability to text dogs our whereabouts, things might quickly improve!)

The reason I want to highlight this is that not everyone understands the underlying terror that is being experienced, particularly not all dog owners. Many times a dog guardian is contacting us because they want to stop the barking due to landlord pressures, or because they want the destruction to stop (very expensive!), or because the dog is eliminating in the house and that is just a terrible mess (and smell) to try and clean up every day. These are all strong motivations, and I commiserate with them.

These guardians have a good point. They need the problem behavior to stop, but is it really the barking, destruction, or elimination that is the dog's exact problem? No. These symptoms are the outward manifestation of an inward anxiety issue. Understanding that these behaviors are a result of fear, and being able to communicate this effectively to clients, is fundamental to gathering empathy for the dog and being effective in resolving the issue.

Show empathy toward your clients and their dogs

Having empathy is essential with this condition for many reasons, but predominantly because the treatment process will likely be arduous. Having that deep-rooted empathy for the dog's overall emotional well-being will help clients persevere. Being patient with the gradual training process requires a genuine understanding of what the dog is experiencing. Tackling daily difficulties is far easier when there is a real incentive. Coming from a place of empathy about their dog's welfare is what can often carry owners to continue with a protocol. This will likely take them much further than just the threat of destruction, vocalization, or elimination. After all, love and compassion are powerful motivators.

Give your client unwavering and compassionate support

The main ingredient for successful treatment of separation anxiety is unwavering and compassionate support from a skilled trainer. Remember, owners of a separation anxiety dog will know nothing about how to overcome the problem. They have no frame of reference, no prior experience (most likely), and no behavior modification protocols to which they can relate. They find it unfathomable that the one- or two-minute absences you will ask them to work on could ever translate into the dog being able to cope with multiple-hour absences. The gradual process of this type of protocol is challenging for most owners and, without reliable guidance from a dog professional, few can stay the course successfully.

The treatment protocols I recommend are time-intensive and require the owners to commit a substantial amount of effort to not leaving their dog alone. For separation anxiety treatment to be successful, you must be not only patient but willing to work closely with guardians without getting frustrated with them or with the training process itself. You have to cheerlead, empathize, support, and encourage, and find new and creative ways to explain and approach problems to break through plateaus. You must be able to discover and point out the incremental progress made, so the client's motivation doesn't falter. You must be hands on with your clients, because a program like this can't simply be handed over to the owners without support. If you do that, they won't succeed.

Client communication

We have already reviewed some strategies for discussing management with clients in Chapter 2. However, I need to emphasize that client counseling, in general, is a skill that can and should be practiced. It takes practice to get proficient with all sorts of communications. Discussing management is one aspect that is so important to helping your client that I recommend lots of rehearsal to achieve competence in your explanation. In our Separation Anxiety Certification Program, we go through considerable rehearsal of the management discussion. We determine the most comfortable and successful ways that each individual student can talk about it. I won't rehash the management discussion again, but I will remind you that getting a commitment from your clients about suspending absences is one of the first requirements for a successful outcome.

Once your client has agreed to move forward with management and training, a different set of communication skills is essential. First and foremost, you need to learn how to initially and continuously set appropriate expectations with your client. Often owners set out treating the issue with great enthusiasm and work on exercises diligently for a while, only to dwindle in their resolve over time because they don't see the results they expected. We trainers must accept our fair share of responsibility for this. Clearly, we need to manage our clients' expectations better. No, they won't be putting on their dancing shoes by next weekend – or even in a few weeks – unless they have a dog sitter. While empathy and diplomacy are keys to successful consultations with distressed owners, sugarcoating the problem or the process involved is a bad idea. The treatment might take a few months or even longer.

Expectations for a client most often revolve around the pacing of the separation anxiety protocol, and it is the dog professional's job to help the client stay motivated. One great way to maintain enthusiasm with training is by cheerleading successes along the way and even setting small attainable goals that are worthy of celebration. Sending a cute meme when the dog hits a full one-minute absence duration for the first time is priceless. Conversely, sending an inspirational quote when the dog is hitting a road bump can be just the needed encouragement.

If you choose to set goals, they must be achievable along the way, and I suggest that they not be number-driven. We can get mired in the numbers at times when other positive things are happening. Conversely, we don't want the client to get number-driven to the point that they want to ignore signs of trouble. Examples of some goals might be that the client can walk across the street to pick up the mail, can drive the car out of sight for the first time, has enough time to get to the nearest café to get a coffee to go, and so on. Notice that I did not suggest that you set a goal in minute increments. These real-life activities are far more worthy of celebration and will work as a positive incentive.

I mentioned empathy above, and I want to let you know a secret about it. If I had to choose one attribute that I feel is most important for someone working with separation anxiety clients, it's empathy. Yes, understanding the specifics of creating a protocol and adjusting criteria carefully are paramount, but these clients need you for more than just that.

Going through separation anxiety is hard work, and it can be an emotional process. There are naysayers at every turn, and clients can feel very isolated. Be there for them, cheer with them, and listen to their woes during times of apprehension.

Using the correct terminology

I mentioned this briefly earlier in the book, but I want to emphasize it again. This book is intended for dog professionals who will be working with separation anxiety clients. If you are a dog owner and wish to work on your separation anxiety training alone, I encourage you to research any unclear terms. I have tried not to use slang in this book, but sometimes it just slips out. There are many dog professionals available to support you if you need help.

This is a brief list of terms that we continually use throughout this book. I have provided definitions here for ease of use.

Absence: The state of being away or not being present. We use a few terms that encompass the different aspects of absences. These are broken down and further defined below.

Absence duration: Length of time the guardian is out of the house (timing begins when the exit door is closed and stops when the exit door is opened).

Absence management: A strategy used in suspending absences in order to never leave the dog home alone for longer than he can handle without experiencing anxiety.

Absence plan or absence rehearsal: See Mission.

Behavior plan: See Mission

Criteria: The standard by which something is judged or assessed; in separation anxiety, it's the level of difficulty of the individual step within the absence plan. Criteria decisions can be based on the duration of the absence or the inclusion (or absence) of a trigger.

Mission: The bundle of individual desensitization steps (depending on the dog's response) designed for the guardian to follow with their dog. The guardian rehearses these five days a week and typically for about 30 minutes of duration. These steps can include pre-departure cues and all aspects that will be included in a particular day's training. Steps and exercises are the individual planned activities within the mission.

Desensitization: A technique whereby a fear-evoking stimulus is presented at an intensity that elicits no fear and is then gradually increased, provided the subject continues to show no fear. In separation anxiety, we typically have to work on desensitizing dogs not only to our actual absence but also to many of the steps surrounding our departure (also known as triggers).

Sensitization: The process of becoming responsive to a given stimulus that previously had no effect or significance. In separation anxiety, when we refer to sensitization, we are referring to a worsening of symptoms, or an increase in reaction to triggers related to being left alone.

Symptoms: Physical or mental features that are regarded as indicating a condition of well-being or lack thereof. In separation anxiety, the symptoms we often see are destruction, vocalization, pacing, panting, drooling, anorexia (not eating when alone), defecation/urination, and self-harm. You may also hear symptoms referred to as anxiety indicators, signs, or displays.

Threshold: The point at which the dog won't recover if he continues to be exposed to a stimulus (in our case, being alone). Every dog's threshold-approaching behavior and body language looks different. There are three terms we'll talk about in the book: under threshold, threshold, and over threshold. (These refer to below, at, or above the threshold.)

Triggers: Individual sights and sounds the dog experiences that cause anxiety or increase anxiety about other stressors. We commonly refer to pre-departure cues as triggers. It is important to note that almost anything can be a trigger. Obvious items like picking up the keys is a trigger, but more obscure triggers also play a role, such as the time of day an absence begins.

Regression: After the dog has made progress, a regression is a reduction in the length of time the dog appears comfortable after the guardians exit the residence. Regressions are normal! Think of them as just pieces of information that will help you move forward.

Village: The support system for the client, which consists of the trainer, friends, family, and community members who help with managing absences. They also are those who listen with an empathetic ear when the client needs to vent. It takes a village!

Using technology to observe dogs during alone time

Whether doing the initial assessment or watching during regular absence rehearsals, we need a way to observe the dog. My personal separation anxiety practice changed dramatically a handful of years ago when smartphones started to have apps that would allow us to watch the dog in real time. This was a complete game-changer for separation anxiety training.

Before the advent of this technology, I would lug my ginormous video camera to the client's house and set it up for them. At the end of the week, I would collect the analog 8mm tapes (yes, I've been doing this *that* long). I would review the recordings and determine whether we were pushing too much or not enough. I was doing all of this after the absences had occurred, so we were making a lot of guesses and hence a lot of errors. At that time, training was reactive versus proactive. Now that we can watch the dog live, things are radically different. We can work in real time. Real-time absence viewing means that we can react before or at the point where we think the dog is starting to show concern – their threshold. We can even set up multiple devices to see numerous angles or various rooms. This is great for some environments – not necessary, but preferred when possible.

I want to walk through just a few technology applications I currently suggest. In my previous book, I talked about several programs, and now many of those are obsolete; that's not surprising since technology advances quickly.

Most of you are familiar with Skype, as it has been a mainstay for technology communications that allow for face-to-face viewing. Skype is a good option for some, as it is so readily available and easy to use. I won't go into great detail on using Skype, because I actually think for these purposes there is something a bit better, but if you are a big Skype user, by all means, continue.

All of the CSATs and I are avid users of Zoom. (See Zoom.us for more detailed information.) Zoom is far more powerful than we need it to be, but it has everything one would want to watch a separation anxiety dog live. The trainer can log in to a Zoom meeting room with the client and watch their dog when the client leaves. The guardian can also use Zoom easily to watch the dog from their smartphone. I cannot express what great fans we are of this platform! (Other programs will likely arise in the future, but at time of publication, Zoom is undeniably our favorite.)

Zoom has a free version that allows unlimited use on one-to-one meetings but also gives 40 minutes free for group meetings of three cameras or more. If you are using multiple cameras, the paid version is really worth it, in my opinion.

Some of the features that make Zoom so appealing are simple, others more robust. First of all, the picture quality is excellent, and we rarely get that garbled image or have a dropped call. All that is required is internet access, and you are good to go. If you are afraid of technology, you will be thrilled with how easy Zoom is to use!

While numerous cameras and applications can be used for these purposes, I won't even try to delve into them all, mainly since newer ones are coming on the market almost daily. As long as the trainer and the client can view the dog in real time, the system you use is a good choice. (See below for further discussion on cameras.)

Technology and benefits of remote training
When I published my first book, it was a surprise and sometimes even a disappointment for people to discover that I conducted separation anxiety training remotely. I suspect there is much less disagreement about this concept now since there are so many services available remotely, including physicians and therapists for human conditions.

Unlike some training protocols, separation anxiety doesn't require the physical presence of the trainer. The trainer's presence can actually inhibit progress by changing the ordinary, everyday circumstances the dog is used to. The "trainer effect," as it's called, often produces false results – dogs seem to be getting better, but only while the trainer is there. Once she leaves, it's back to anxiety as usual. With remote training, clients get all the trainer support without the trainer effect, which means they get to keep the results gained.

Moreover, with separation anxiety, we as dog professionals get to be a fly on the wall when using remote tools. Due to the way that technology has evolved, it is far superior to work with SA clients online than in person. These days, when the occasional client asks if I would be willing to meet in person, I am not only surprised, but I am at a slight loss for how to answer. Meeting the client and their dog in person is always lovely, and I cherish these interactions immensely, of course. With technology, though, we can view the dog in real time in their normal, unencumbered environment. We can watch all of the subtle signs of anxiety in the dog. We can keep track of the client's activities as they get ready to leave while we maintain data on the dog's displayed behaviors. We can also counsel the online client face-to-face even when they live miles or continents away.

There are so many benefits of training remotely that I cannot imagine any benefits of in-person separation anxiety at this point unless you are a veterinarian and need to do a physical workup.

Cottam et al. (2008) found no difference between the effectiveness of behavioral advice for canine separation anxiety when it was delivered in person, by phone, or by email, suggesting that the medium by which advice is delivered is unimportant.

Here are just a few more of the benefits of remote training:

Scheduling: You can schedule training time that works easily for both you and the client. This also allows you to work with clients outside of your immediate area. Whether the client is across town or in a different time zone, you can work the scheduling to suit both of you.

Cost and efficiency: Instead of spending wasted time in traffic or commuting, you can meet with the client from wherever you are, typically from your home office, but wherever you and your computer are will do. Instead of needing to do an appointment of an hour or more, you can conduct a meeting for only the time required. Between eliminating commute time and keeping appointment times to a minimum, you can either gain more revenue for your time or choose to pass on some savings to the client if you prefer.

Best possible results: Because of your time/cost savings, and due to the various ways that you can create client packages, you can provide extremely individualized regular support. We support our clients five days a week, and I cannot begin to express the impact that this has on reaching successful outcomes.

Client compliance: The continued counseling and cheerleading, combined with the accountability and expert coaching that clients receive, means that compliance goes through the roof. Clients who are left to their own devices on their separation anxiety training will rarely make the same level of progress, especially in the beginning stages. If you are a trainer who typically bemoans client compliance, you are going to love separation anxiety clients!

Body language reading education: Not all clients can stick with their trainer day-to-day for the duration of their dog's protocol. For those who have to go on their own after a time, we can equip them with skillful knowledge on reading their own dog's body language.

Data tracking: Using online resources, we can carefully track the daily fluctuations and influences that are affecting the dog during their separation anxiety protocol. I will go into this in more detail in the next section, but for now, you should know that the results have been statistically impressive with dogs, even when compared to just ten years ago, when online tracking tools and live viewing platforms were not available.

Since we are talking nerdy here, I'll switch gears slightly into one last piece of technology. You've already read about Zoom, which is our preferred method of viewing the client and dog, but I don't want to skip over the fact that there are some outstanding stand-alone cameras and some excellent phone apps that can also be used. These typically allow for even more detailed viewing.

As a quick explanation, there are three categories to choose from when viewing a dog during an absence (you can certainly combine types as well):

- **Online platforms:** These are typically free or low-cost programs that you can use online. Some of the most commonly used are Zoom, Skype, FaceTime, and Google Hangouts.

- **Stand-alone cameras:** These are cameras that you can purchase that will allow you to view the dog live. They range in price from reasonable to expensive, depending on your preference. Some of the most commonly used and recommended by us at time of publication are Yi1080P, Nest (formerly DropCam), and Amcrest (either the 1080P or the wide angle are great).

- **Apps:** These are apps available in the App Store on your iOS or Android device that are typically free or very low-cost. Some of our favorites and recommended by us at time of publication are Presence and iCam.

By whatever method, I urge you to have some way to view the dog during the absence. Long ago, when I didn't have the technology to watch the dog live, my success rate was much lower, and the process of setting regular criteria was much more challenging.

Two bits of counsel about stand-alone cameras or apps that are available.

1. We don't recommend using a two-way microphone to speak to the dog remotely. Most dogs won't attend to a voice over an audio speaker in the first place. In the rare event that they might, this practice could actually cause problems rather than be helpful. Remember that we are teaching the dog to be comfortable being alone. That means the client is not present in any way.

2. While there are numerous camera options that also allow for treat dispensing, we don't recommend using that feature when desensitizing a separation anxiety dog to absences. The cameras with that function are fun, and I love that people are thinking about their dogs at home, but they are not applicable for SA training.

As a final note, if you are technologically challenged, don't worry! Depending on where you live, there are often computer geeks for hire who can help you set things up. While a computer professional is great support, most of us have a youngster amongst our friends and family who can whiz through the setup of any of these technologies (think kids around 8 years of age or older).

Tracking data

Before we get too deep into this nerdy section, I want to let you know that if you are not into numbers, spreadsheets, or general technology, it's OK. There are varying degrees of sophistication and difficulty that you can incorporate into your separation anxiety protocols, including those as simple as a notebook and pen or fancy formulas in an online spreadsheet.

I am a science geek. What I do with separation anxiety is based on scientific principles and research. I love data and discerning what that data can tell me or do to help a separation anxiety dog. (Before my career in dog training, I was actually a statistician, so data crunching is in my DNA, I suppose.)

While executing a separation anxiety protocol is mostly about efficiently monitoring body language to create daily training exercises (missions), numerous variables can, and often do affect the individual dog. These variables should be considered when generating a plan.

A simple example of this is as follows:

Fluffy's threshold is 12 minutes. Her guardians usually do their mission in the late morning sometime before noon because that is the best time for their scheduling. One day, Fluffy's owners have a jumbled schedule, and they do her mission at 6 p.m. They follow their mission as written, but Fluffy doesn't do nearly as well as she had been doing previously. There are a few things we could consider here:

- Did Fluffy just have an off day?
- Was there some sort of event that occurred that day that added to Fluffy's stress?
- Is Fluffy more sensitive to evening departures than she is to morning departures?
- Do Fluffy's parents have slightly different pre-departure cues for nighttime absences (for example, no sunglasses and different shoes)?
- Is it possible that this off day is the beginning of a regression?

These are just some of the questions you might be asking yourself about the absence rehearsal done that evening, and you wouldn't have a clear answer to whether all or any of these were factors.

Because there are so many variables in each absence rehearsal that are unique to each dog and household, it is incredibly shrewd to track some data so that you can begin to discern patterns. Each client might have a different set of data that you will follow, but some commonalities are always worthwhile to track, such as the time of day the absence is done or the amount of exercise the dog received during each day.

The way I instruct the CSATs to track client data is uncomplicated, but we can make it even simpler if you prefer. At the most basic level, jotting down a few details in a notebook or on the calendar can be useful. This way is not as powerful, because it's harder to see patterns, but it is sufficient.

The way that CSATs track data is through using spreadsheets, and I highly recommend you use an online spreadsheet such as Google Sheets so that you can interactively share it with your client.

Here is a simple example of a spreadsheet with some sample data in it:

Data Tracking Sorted by Mission Number

Mission #	Mission Date	Mission Time	Final Duration	Person(s)	Feeding Time	Exercise in min.	Environmental Influences	Mission Rating
1	1/4	6:15 am	5	P	6:45 am	30	Vet visit	2
2	1/5	10:30 am	9	C	7:10 am	60	None	1
3	1/6	9:00 am	6	CP	7:00 am	0	Construction noise	3
4	1/7	6:45 am	10	CP	7:15 am	15	Raining	3
5	1/8	7:00 am	13	C	7:45 am	45	None	1
6	1/11	8:45 am	9	C	7:30 am	60	None	1
7	1/12	8:00 am	8	CP	7:00 am	15	Thunderstorm	3
8	1/13	10:45 am	15	C	6:00 am	45	None	1
9	1/14	7:00 am	19	P	7:45 am	30	Windy	2
10	1/15	9:30 am	12	P	8:00 am	30	Passed Reactive Dog	1

Legend: 1 = Great, 2 = Good, 3 = Fair

When using spreadsheets like this, I suggest that the date (or number) of the mission goes down the first column and that the variables (or parameters) go across the columns to the right.

You'll see in the example spreadsheet that we are tracking the following parameters: Mission Number, Mission Date, Mission Time (of day), Final Duration (in the mission), Person(s) Doing the Mission, Feeding Time, Exercise in Minutes, Environmental Influences, and Mission Rating.

One of those parameters is a rating scale. You can choose whatever rating scale you like, but it should indicate how the dog did with that day's mission as closely as possible. The rating scale can be as simple as Good, Fair, or Poor, or it can be as complicated as using the numbers 1 through 4 and explicitly defining what each of those numbers represents in terms of specific, observable behavior for a given dog.

An example of a rating scale is as follows. *Please* remember this is for a specific dog and would not apply to any dog but Fluffy.

Example of a simple legend

Rating	General Descriptor	Detailed Examples of Rating Description
1	Great	No whining or pawing
2	Good	Brief whining or pawing once at door
3	Fair	Some mild vocalization and pawing more than once at the door

When your client has completed only a handful of missions, the data may not show much in the way of patterns, but as you move forward and gather more information, helpful correlations can often emerge.

In computerized spreadsheets, you can quickly sort the data by any factor to see if it is affecting the daily missions in any way (positively or negatively).

For example, in the chart on the next page, you will see the same information that was in Image 1, except it is sorted by Mission Rating. When arranged like this, you can see that there are various factors affecting the missions, including amount of exercise, who was doing the mission, and external noises that are listed under Environmental Influences. For example, do you see that the person doing the mission is sometimes C (Chris) alone, sometimes P (Pat) alone, and sometimes the two of them together? That is often a parameter that can influence the dog, and here we do see that when Chris is doing the missions, they are better than when Pat alone does missions. When the two of them exit together, the missions do not go nearly as well. Additionally, when there has been minimal exercise or when there are outside noises like storms or construction noise, Fluffy's alone-time tolerance is affected. At this point we would want to test these various parameters to see if we could adjust criteria surrounding them. We would ensure that we maintained at least 30 minutes of exercise and we would evaluate if there were steps to take to minimize external noises, such as a white noise machine. Finally, we would adjust the criteria carefully depending on who was conducting the mission.

Data Tracking Sorted by Mission Rating

Mission #	Mission Date	Mission Time	Final Duration	Person(s)	Feeding Time	Exercise in min.	Environmental Influences	Mission Rating
2	1/5	10:30 am	9	C	7:10 am	60	None	1
5	1/8	7:00 am	13	C	7:45 am	45	None	1
6	1/11	8:45 am	9	C	7:30 am	60	None	1
8	1/13	10:45 am	15	C	6:00 am	45	None	1
10	1/15	9:30 am	12	P	8:00 am	30	Passed Reactive Dog	1
1	1/4	6:15 am	5	P	6:45 am	30	Vet visit	2
9	1/14	7:00 am	19	P	7:45 am	30	Windy	2
3	1/6	9:00 am	6	CP	7:00 am	0	Construction noise	3
4	1/7	6:45 am	10	CP	7:15 am	15	Raining	3
7	1/12	8:00 am	8	CP	7:00 am	15	Thunderstorm	3

Legend: 1 = Great, 2 = Good, 3 = Fair

I won't get too nerded-out on all the possibilities with tracking, but do know that you can sort your data in many, many ways, and track multiple parameters to guide you.

The last thing I'll mention about data tracking is that it can also be a form of motivation for you and the client. We can periodically generate graphs that show the dog's progress over time or charts that show the percentages of absences that were rated high.

Two example graphs are shown here:

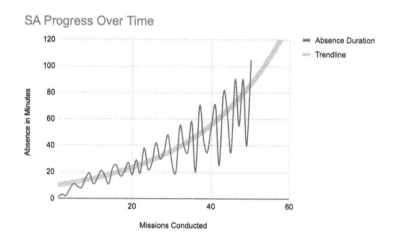

SA Progress Over Time

The first image is similar to the graph you saw earlier in the book. It is charting progress over time, and it even generates a trendline that can not only be inspiring but can also help us judge how to further set criteria based on performance. The pie chart is another example of a graph that helps with inspiration and also allows for some decision making. You'll see that 50% of the missions conducted received a rating of great, and another 36% received a rating of good. That is well over 80% of missions that the dog performed well. Exciting! If you are not accomplishing at least 50% of missions with a great or at least good rating, then it is time to adjust criteria in the protocol to help the dog perform better.

I can't express enough how valuable tracking your data can be. There have been many times that we have been able to truly propel the training forward due to the information that we discerned from our data tracking. Common parameters that influence a protocol are time of day and the person or persons doing the mission. Watch those carefully and keep track of environmental influences as well. Setting the dog up for success is the key to getting to the finish line most efficiently.

Time commitment

The amount of time that we, as CSATs, devote to our one-to-one clients is considerable (five days a week of training support). There are several reasons for this.

First of all, the client is not going to be nearly as savvy as we are in observing and interpreting body language. Many of our clients start out saying things like, "I saw her wagging her tail for a few moments during the absence, so she must be happy." As a dog professional, you know that a wagging tail is not always a sign of glee, and the client's misinterpretation of this or other body indicators could make a tremendous difference in how the daily missions are created.

Additionally, yet no less importantly, when the dog is your own, it is all too common to let emotions cloud judgment. I know this personally as I went through a separation anxiety protocol with my own dog, and I was an absolute emotional wreck when attempting to determine her threshold. (She has recovered, in case you were wondering!)

Some clients are so worried about every little whine and mini-movement that they are afraid to push forward, but it's more typical for clients to either overlook or ignore some of the indicators. These clients would push too quickly on their own if not guided.

There are other essential reasons to have very regular communication with your clients, including maintaining accountability, helping with motivation, and attending to emotional swings. This stuff can be trying for many people; the slightest gain can make people's emotions soar high while the merest regression can plummet one's faith and enthusiasm. Working a separation anxiety protocol is a lonely venture for some, as there are typically people amongst the client's family, friends, colleagues, and social media contacts who are nay-saying every action. Don't let your clients become waylaid by these outsiders; they must stay the course with resilience, and you are there to help them remain strong.

Finally, the need to vary the duration and difficulty is not natural for people to execute. Randomization is not particularly innate to humans, and clients are incredibly prone to want the trajectory to be continually increasing. That's OK; it's a human condition to want to get hard work over quickly, but moving in a straight line of difficulty can be disastrous for the dog and can cause sensitization. It's crucially important to make sure you are mixing it up for the client by writing easier missions some days, and other days creating medium or hard missions.

We work with our clients five days a week, wherein one of the days is an online reassessment (live), and on the other days we communicate by sending the new mission for that day via the Google Sheet.

Yes, this sounds intense and is likely much more time than you might need for other training issues, but it is highly advised as the optimal way to support your client.

While each practitioner will have a different speed at which they work, when working with clients five days a week, we are typically devoting a total of two to three hours a week to each client. In the beginning, when first working with separation anxiety, it can take a little extra time to create regular missions, but as one gains expertise, the amount of daily time devoted reduces, hence the two to three hour a week trainer commitment. During the Separation Anxiety Certification Program, we allocate significant time to working on mission creation and reading dog body language. Even after graduation, CSATs aren't speeding through mission-writing straightaway, so know it really does take practice.

As you all know, this profession is unregulated, and I feel strongly that professionals who are educationally accomplished and proficient in their practice should be remunerated suitably. I know personally how much time, devotion, and money expenditure it has taken me (and the CSATs) to develop expertise in the field of dog training, and that is extremely valuable. The difference between a novice guardian trying to execute a daily separation anxiety protocol and a competent professional doing so is dramatic.

Confidence and thorough understanding of the process

Having confidence in yourself, in the training protocol, in the owner, and in the dog is a quintessential part of working with separation anxiety clients. I honestly cannot repeat this enough.

We have to remember that you, as the professional, have a view of training and behavior that allows you to understand the inner workings of desensitization, while the client, on the other hand, does not. The average owner has no way to grasp that a shaky starting absence of 20 seconds can in time develop into a four-hour comfortable absence for their dog. These clients, therefore, heavily rely on you to guide them, and your conviction of direction will help their faith in the process grow along the way.

To have conviction in your direction and confidence in everything about the protocol, a thorough understanding of the process is required. I won't hide the fact that not only have I experienced self-doubt during protocols, but I have discussed this familiar sentiment with CSATs as well. We are human, after all, and when training moves this slowly with hiccups along the way, we are bound to feel occasional uncertainty.

It gets better as you work with more cases. That is one guarantee that I can make to you. When you see the process work time and time again, your sureness will swell. But do know that when working with clients that are justifiably filled with worry, it is not always easy to avoid occasional feelings of misgiving yourself.

Ability to read body language well

As a dog professional, I suspect that if you are not already an expert-level reader of body language, it is your goal to become one. Understanding and using body indicators to support any type of training is critical. Indiscriminately pushing an uncomfortable dog during training is a mistake, whether that be for separation anxiety or in teaching a simple sit. All training should consider the dog's body language, as it is the critical clue to understanding the learner.

When working with a separation anxiety dog, there are unlimited types of body indicators that can be observed, and no two dogs express their anxiety in precisely the same way. From the 10,000-foot view, you could say, well, both of these dogs vocalize when left alone. But we need to look at the granular view to identify the detail. Those same two vocalizing dogs have individually diverse characteristics (physiognomies) that comprise their anxiety display.

The list of indications of anxiety and precursors to stress one might look for is endless. Because of the limitless body language possibilities, I hesitate to provide a hasty inventory, so I hope a few examples and explanations are helpful before referring to the basic list I provide below. This chart shows the prevalence of certain behaviors in a cohort of dogs diagnosed with separation anxiety and a control group without SA.

Risk Factors Chart

Behavior	SA dogs (%)	Non-SA dogs (%)
Destruction	72	3
Vocalization	61	5
Elimination	28	2
Shadowing or following owner closely	84	64
Signs when owner puts on coat or shoes	70	32
Excessive greeting upon owner's return	63	31
Disinterest in eating when alone	47	21
Behavioral signs of depression	59	16
Drooling excessively/vomiting/ diarrhea	20	0

Flannigan, Gerrard, and Nicholas H. Dodman. "Risk factors and behaviors associated with separation anxiety in dogs." Journal of the American Veterinary Medical Association 219.4 (2001): 460-466.

We commonly see indicators such as lip licking, yawning, mild pacing, or vigilant attention as precursors to other more recognizable anxiety behaviors like barking or pawing at exits. Not only are no two dogs alike in their unique presentation, no two symptoms are equal in their own right either. In other words, sometimes a yawn is indicative of a tired or relaxed dog, so viewing the entire dog and all his body language is vital to allow for context.

I personally like to get a baseline knowledge of the dog's behavior when he is relaxed at home while not alone. If he is a dog who frequently licks his lips in non-stressful, contented environments, I won't put nearly the same weight on that behavior when alone as I would for a dog who rarely or never licked his lips in the absence of stress. This would be true of many actions such as yawning, vigilant attention, scratching oneself (displacement versus being itchy), and even ambulatory behaviors like mild pacing.

Some symptoms aren't ambiguous. Most any alone-time indicator that is physically involuntary should be viewed as a noteworthy sign of anxiety.

The most common alone-time examples of involuntary behaviors are hyper-salivation, sweaty paws, abrupt shedding, and even elimination (urination or defecation). Note the frequency of salivation, diarrhea, and vomiting by SA dogs in the chart above. Gastrointestinal issues like vomiting and diarrhea could be connected to any number of medical conditions. Drooling can be linked to GI distress, or even be connected to oral or dental problems. If these things happen exclusively when the dog is alone, then that may point toward separation anxiety. But behavior consultants are not veterinarians, and we can't diagnose, nor can we rule out medical reasons for distressed behaviors. So, this is but one of the many times I will emphasize the importance of a thorough vet check for any separation anxiety dog.

Sometimes the observable symptoms (particularly precursor ones) are incredibly subtle. For the most part, once you have observed a dog a few times in assessments and reassessments, you can piece together the signs that their anxiety is escalating and pinpoint a few symptoms that indicate the dog is at or approaching their threshold. Again, the indicators are individual to the dog.

We also must remind ourselves that correlation does not equal causation. Correlation between two events or variables merely indicates that a relationship exists. Causation means that one event actually caused the other. Lists of possible stress behaviors and their frequency are helpful, but we need to be careful about our assumptions. The behavior listed in the chart of "shadowing or following owner closely" provides a cautionary example. It has sometimes been erroneously extrapolated that dogs who follow their owners closely suffer from separation anxiety. This deduction is sometimes further used to infer that separation anxiety is therefore caused by owner attachment.

Looking back at the risk factors chart on page 65, it is apparent that there may be some flawed arguments occurring when using owner-following behavior to conclude an attachment theory. Reviewing line 4 of that chart, "Shadowing or following owner closely," we can see that 84% of separation anxiety dogs did indeed follow their owners closely. However, 64% of non-SA dogs also followed their owners closely. Seeing the high incidence of this behavior in both separation anxiety and non-separation anxiety dogs weakens the causation argument for the SA dogs.

On occasion, it is a little trickier to identify what the dog's nuanced behaviors are that show his distress. One example that I think of often is a dog we worked with long ago. He was an all-black dog, which in and of itself makes body language a little harder to interpret, since the lighting doesn't always pick up the details of black dogs. In this case, the dog (Charlie) would go to the door and lie down shortly after the guardians would exit. Sometimes his head was down, sometimes up, but overall his body language did appear relaxed (hip to one side and supple in appearance overall).

After a short while, it appeared that Charlie would just suddenly break into mournful howls. While it appeared that the howling indicated distress, we could not determine anything that occurred before the howl to help us predict what was coming.

I definitely prefer to end a session before this sort of howling begins, so we were a bit stumped. After several live reviews of the dog, we decided to record the absence and watch it in slow motion; darned if that didn't give us the answers we were looking for. When viewing in slow motion, it is sometimes easier to see the sequence of body language indicators and determine what happens before an overt sign like howling.

Before the howling, Charlie's head would be raised (but it was up at other times as well). What we noticed in the slow-motion video was that before Charlie began to howl, he twitched his ears backward and forward several times. I can guarantee that this was not Charlie just hearing a noise, if that's what you are thinking. His ear twitching was clearly related to the length of the absence and always directly preceded his mournful vocalization. Subtle as it was, once we noticed this in slow motion, it was unmistakably apparent in every absence, which gave us our answer. When we began to see ear twitching, we knew a howl would follow soon, so our threshold was readily identified. From that point forward, it was easy to pinpoint the time we should have the guardian return, and the protocol moved forward much more smoothly.

Be diligent about finding those body cues; it's rare that there is no indicator.

Hopefully, with the explanations above, you understand that the following list of body language indicators is not universal but is restrictive if you don't look at the individual dog in his entirety.

Potential Anxiety Indicators

- Avoiding eye contact
- Barking/Howling/ Whining
- Trembling or shaking
- Clinging to the owner
- Nose licking
- Defecation
- Urination/ Dribbling
- Escaping
- Furrowed Brows
- Freezing or walking slowly
- Ears Lowered/ Flattened
- Growling/ aggression
- "Whale Eye" or Staring

- Mouth pursed forward
- Overly "Excited" whiskers
- Nipping out of context
- Starting easily at changes/noises
- Self mutilation
- Hiding
- Decreased/ Increased eating
- Hyper-salivation
- Hyper-vigilance
- Panting
- Piloerection (raised hair)
- Rigid or forward stance
- Destruction/door scratching

- Anal sac expression
- Increased heart rate
- Blinking or squinting
- Increased grooming
- Cowering
- Yawning
- Increased activity (pacing)
- Dilated pupils
- Lifting paw
- Lip licking
- Repetitive behaviors
- Increased reactivity
- Mouth closed tightly/pulled back

Training knowledge

As a dog professional, if you are treating any type of behavior issue, you must understand learning principles. For separation anxiety, having detailed knowledge of what desensitization is and knowing which antecedent arrangements are potentially influencing your protocol are both imperative.

I have already touched on desensitization earlier in the book, but it bears explaining a bit further. As mentioned, gradually increasing increments of exposure and repetition of those is what makes up a reliable desensitization protocol.

Your job is to instruct the client on how to move forward with the repetitions of their protocol slowly. I emphasize the word slowly here because, understandably, clients tend to want to move faster than is typically recommended for their dog. Of course they would, since it seems that moving along at a more rapid pace and pushing often would help get to the finish line more quickly. This is unquestionably not the case. In her recently published study on separation anxiety training, Erica Feuerbacher notes that the dog in the study who had the highest percentage of successful trials also had an owner who increased the departure duration the slowest and had the greatest number of short departures. The authors concluded that systematic desensitization was the critical component for successful treatment and that counterconditioning and other behavioral advice did not influence the behavioral outcome (2020).

Slow is the new fast.

If you think you are going slowly enough, slow down a bit, and that is probably going to be the appropriate speed.

Going at the dog's pace is often very hard for us humans, who are used to things happening at tech-speed, but it's absolutely imperative that the dog is in the driver's seat and that we work at the dog's natural or biological speed and are sensitive to their needs, rather than give in to our desire to go fast.

Desensitizing dogs to being alone
Straightforward desensitization is the most potent tool to use in your efforts to condition the dog to being alone and is the central training method around which your behavior and training plans are designed. In dog training, it is commonplace to combine desensitization with counter-conditioning, so we often default to these two working together, like peanut butter and jelly. They do work independently,

though, and you can make a proper sandwich out of just peanut butter, so to speak.

Desensitization is a process by which the dog is introduced to the scary stimulus (alone time) in extremely small increments keeping the dog under threshold at all times. The threshold is defined as the point at which the dog is not yet experiencing anxiety, but where they may be just starting to get disquieted. To be clear, with counter-conditioning, we introduce a rewarding stimulus such as food to create a positive association with the scary stimulus. For most behaviors, when counter-conditioning is used correctly, it is a powerful adjunct to desensitization. With separation anxiety, the counter-conditioning piece can be counterproductive.

I will be going through an example training plan later in Chapter 5 but do know that the key to separation anxiety training is gradually increasing increments and repetition. It is a rare occurrence when we are actually trying to get our dogs bored in life...bored is a bad thing for dogs, right? Indeed, in separation anxiety training, boring is a good thing. We want the dog to feel that the owner repeatedly leaving home and coming back is the most boring thing ever, so he will just hang out and possibly even nap.

Exits and returns
The first several repetitions of exiting the door will be ever-so-brief for most dogs. We want the dog to feel totally comfortable with our exits and returns, so even just a mere second (or less) of being out the door will be enough to start this "game." Once the dog has successfully navigated a full second of alone time, we can then begin to increase the duration in tiny increments. One thing to keep in mind, though, is that we want to *move variably*. By variably, I mean that sometimes the absence duration will be random: sometimes short, sometimes long, and sometimes medium in length. Short, long, and medium are determined by where the dog is currently successful in terms of duration (threshold).

Using this fluctuating duration is vital for several reasons. Dogs are highly observant, pattern-seeking missiles. If every absence is longer than the last, even if by tiny increments, the dog could figure out the game, determining that it is getting increasingly stressful. This could potentially lead to sensitization. We need to include some "easy wins" in each mission to avoid an unrelenting increase of difficulty. And dogs are not the only ones who fall into patterns. If left to our own devices, humans fall into patterns as well. Most of us can't create a set of random durations on the fly, which is why we carefully and purposely write out durations for the client in advance of doing a mission.

So, for example, if you are working on absences of mere seconds, the longest one might be three seconds, and the shortest one might be just stepping out the door and immediately back in. But we won't start stepping out the door and back in, followed by staying out for one second, then two seconds, then three. We will mix them up. Later, as you achieve greater duration, you can make adjustments so that, say, 30 seconds is the longer duration and maybe five seconds is the shorter duration. But the absences will never march linearly from shortest to longest.

Part of executing a successful desensitization protocol is to move as gradually as necessary for the dog to make progress. Moving too quickly can appear to work occasionally; however, what often happens is the dog will suddenly crash later down the line. This crashing seems to be a result of not building an initial foundation with enough resiliency.

Conducting a desensitization protocol is like building a house – if the foundation is cracked or in any way unstable, the house will tumble at some point.

Similar to building a home, the early stages of a separation anxiety protocol are often the most painstaking. Once the foundation is built, the frame goes up, and the work moves quickly through to completion. With SA, after an appreciable foundation of duration is established, the dog can make swift progress.

In addition to understanding desensitization thoroughly, a dog professional needs to have an excellent working knowledge of the importance of antecedent arrangements and also how each potential trigger is affecting their protocol.

What we mean by antecedent arrangements are those items that predict other stimuli. For instance, grabbing the leash typically means the dog gets a walk, so the leash is the antecedent to good times. Conversely, picking up a backpack often leads to an absence. In that example, the cue (picking up the backpack) is predictive of scary stuff for a separation anxiety dog.

A common hiccup that we see in protocols is not incorporating the pre-departure cues (or other triggers) properly. Unlike traditional protocols that encouraged owners to spend lots of time "uncoupling" departure cues, the correct way to integrate such triggers as grabbing the keys or picking up a purse is not to try to remove them from the sequence entirely.

The typical advice suggests that in advance of ever exiting, time should be devoted to unpairing triggers. An example would be picking up the keys and putting them down again or putting on a coat and then going about doing something other than leaving. While I understand the origin of this advice, there is a much more efficient and effective way to work with departure cues. The process of uncoupling cues in advance of ever exiting has a significant fault. If you can get the dog to feel that the cue (say the coat) no longer means that you are leaving, you are eventually going to create a spontaneous recovery of that concern when the coat actually does precede exiting the house, which it must at some point.

This is why it is imperative to understand antecedent arrangements and how they influence your protocol. If grabbing the coat, shoes, keys, or bag is typically going to predict an absence, then we need to integrate these actions into our protocol rather than attempt to train the dog that they do not lead to an absence.

Desensitizing a dog to a brief absence without any of these triggers is the first order of business. If the dog can handle, say, a 30-second absence without the predictive cues, we can then gradually incorporate those cues individually into the protocol. The important thing here is that the dog *first* learns that the brief absence is not scary and *then* begins to learn that the cue (say the coat) leads to this non-scary departure (not the other way around!).

When we discuss mission creation, we'll review more details about adding in cues, but for now, please remember that every time you make an absence harder in some way (such as adding a coat), you must lower the difficulty of the absence in another way, such as by reducing duration. I refer to this as toggling.

To clarify, we would build a dog up to a brief comfortable duration absence (I'll use 30 seconds as an example but know that it can be different for each dog). Once we have that comfortable 30 seconds, we can decide that it is time to introduce the coat. We will put on the jacket and exit for a mere millisecond this time as opposed to again using the 30 seconds.

When you raise one criterion, you must lower another.

In time, putting on the coat becomes a predictor of safe absences, and the time outside can again be increased. At that point, we can add in a new departure cue (say, the keys), but we should remember two things: Be sure to lower the criterion of duration again, and don't always put all departure cues together. You may want to exit with the keys and no coat a handful of times for a brief duration before starting to build up multiple triggers together. Then, in time, you can include the jacket and keys together, but again, lower that duration the first several times during repetitions. On occasion, you should be doing absences with few or no departure cues to help solidify that absences of any type are not scary.

Finally, please remember that dogs are absolute masters of discrimination. Because dogs don't have the language ability that we do, they use environmental cues to discriminate between indicators of "safe" versus "unsafe," and they are incredibly keen at distinguishing patterns of all kinds. If you always do a 15-second absence when you exit with your coat on and always do a 30-second absence when you exit without your coat on, the dog will discern that pattern (and quickly too).

Toggle, toggle, toggle.

Thresholds and body language

Getting to know (and work under) the dog's threshold is the number one aim in separation anxiety training. "Under threshold" is defined as the point at which the dog is still comfortable or not experiencing alone-time anxiety. Over threshold is the point at which the dog begins to exhibit anxiety while being left alone. In her 2013 Pet Professional Guild webinar called "Over-Threshold: The Changing Definition," Eileen Anderson defined threshold as follows: "The point at which an existing stimulus becomes aversive, generally because of the intensity of the exposure." In Jean Donaldson's Pet Professional Guild webinar from 2012 called "The Pitfalls of Negative Reinforcement," she also talks about threshold: "'Under threshold' is an intensity of stimulus that elicits no fear...Not 'mild fear' or 'manageable fear,' it's 'NO fear.'"

Intensity may mean absence duration for a separation anxiety dog, but it could also mean that there are triggers making the absence more difficult, too. Examples of such triggers are dead-bolting the door or hearing the car start. Keeping this in mind, your goal in this part of the management plan is to allow the dog to remain comfortable, not push him to display anxiety responses. Ballantyne (2018) notes that "Throughout this process, it is essential that the intensity of the stimulus is never presented at a level that elicits the fear response or sensitization to the stimulus, and worsening of the fear response rather than desensitization will occur."

Some dogs display signs of anxiety the moment someone even approaches the door. For other dogs, it could take five minutes or more before we see any visible signs of distress. To determine a dog's threshold, we need to get good at observing their body language. Dogs will display various precursors to their mounting anxiety, and this is something we want to become experts at discerning for the individual dog. Additionally, we should have some skill in teaching the client about their individual dog's body language. A guardian's ability to recognize signs of stress is important, as it enables them to avoid welfare problems such as stressful situations by interrupting the progress to distress (Mariti, 2012).

Sunny is a dog who displays the following when left alone:

- She lies on her bed for about 15 to 20 seconds.
- She gets up and investigates the exit door for 30 seconds while calmly sitting.
- She goes to the window and watches (alertly) for one minute.
- She starts to pace a little, then whines a few times softly.
- Finally, when she stops at the door a second time, Sunny will begin to bark, as her anxiety rises and continues to surge.

In this example, we would choose an indicator like "before or at the start of pacing" to set our first limit for the absence rehearsal. We can develop our protocol around knowing these various body language precursors, and with time we will see further relaxation for longer duration. We will detect the dog's new threshold and adjust our protocol to reflect it.

This is but one example; every dog is an individual and will display their anxiety in different ways and at different durations. Remember when I mentioned that I could not give you a specific and detailed written protocol that would be applicable for any dog? This right here is one of the many reasons why.

As we move forward in our protocol, we will carefully observe the dog's body language to discern the proper threshold and where the appropriate intensity of exposure is at any given time.

If Sunny's example seems intensely detailed, it is. As separation anxiety trainers, we take time and lots of practice to learn how to read intricate body language cues and then use them to develop training steps. It becomes second nature to do this after watching separation anxiety dogs day after day, so be patient with your learning curve. Additionally, remember that your ability to observe body language is typically profoundly better than that of the average dog owner. They need your guidance. As a side note, one thing that is influencing the dog owner's ability to accurately read body language is their emotional attachment. It is much harder to view a dog's behavior clinically when you are looking through rose-colored glasses of adoration.

I recently heard an ideal narrative that reminded me of working with a dog's threshold. This example was given by applied animal behaviorist Kathy Sdao, MA, whom I utterly revere. Kathy was talking about training being like sailing. She (like me) is not a sailor; however, the parallel is not lost without that know-how.

Kathy explained that, when sailing, you are constantly observing and regularly adjusting your sail so that you can capture optimal wind concentrations for propulsion. Working with threshold is analogous to sailing in that many factors feed into the speed and direction of the training, and we must constantly adjust. The owner is continuously watching the dog's body language in order to fine-tune the training direction. Watching the dog's body language is a corollary to needing to watch the response of the boat to the wind. While most sailing involves tweaks and mild modifications, on occasion, the wind can change dramatically, and you must accommodate. Dogs can be similar in that moving through a protocol is primarily made up of fiddling and varying, but sometimes a directional change is required.

Forgive me, dear reader, as I play a bit too exuberantly with some sailing phrases that are mysteriously applicable to Kathy's training-is-like-sailing metaphor. In sailing and dog training alike, be mindful of a few of these:

- Don't "sail close to the wind," which is just another way of telling you not to take unnecessary risks or push your luck. While we are at it, let me remind you not to "rock the boat" too often as well. Heedlessly disturbing the training is an error to avoid. Please don't "make waves."

- Failing to adjust to your environment may cause you to "veer off-course" or worse yet, leave you "dead in the water." Fortunately, though, many dog professionals can "throw you a lifeline" if it's ever needed.

- If you stay on the "right tack" and "run a tight ship," you will certainly "turn the corner," so I encourage you to "learn the ropes" and never "abandon ship" entirely. (Note: It is "tack," not "track," in this example, meaning that if the sailor takes the wrong tack or line, they will end up going the wrong direction.)

I hope the image of sailing has helped you glean some understanding of the gradations that can impact training within threshold as I certainly would hate to leave you "all at sea."

Must-haves for guardians

It is likely not a surprise that some of the requirements of dog owners are similar to that of dog pros when working on a separation anxiety protocol.

Ability to commit time to train

We ask our clients to commit to training about five days a week for 20 to 30 minutes each session. There are clients whose outside commitments necessitate that they do less, but this is a suitable base requirement for most. While sometimes clients require training on fewer days, I highly discourage devoting more days or longer duration. (The exception is when the client gets to the point that their dog can stay alone for longer than 30 minutes. At that point there will, of course, be some longer days.)

Separation anxiety training takes consistent practice. Unlike teaching a dog a trick or a sit, which is not a behavior steeped in fear, with SA we are working with anxiety. Careful and systematic training must take place gradually.

When you are working with a client, it is vital to ensure they understand this time commitment. One thing that helps tremendously with this commitment is your continued support and its relationship to accountability for the client.

If your client Sally knows that tomorrow morning you will be looking at her mission notes to generate a new set of training exercises for the day, she may be significantly more motivated not to give in to the beckoning couch that evening and instead do her 20 to 30 minutes of training. Having accountability like this helps most clients stick to their plan.

Speaking of motivation, while we love when our clients are motivated to train and to succeed, it is entirely normal for clients to have days where SA training seems futile and disruptive. Your job is to help them get through those times. Working on such tiny increments can feel fruitless at times, particularly when only the final results are in mind. Having little reasons for celebration along the way can help significantly.

Ability to commit to management

Management has been reviewed already, but its importance can't be overstated. I spend a lot of time with the client discussing the "why" and the "how" of not leaving the dog alone longer than he can handle.

If a client chooses not to uphold this management requirement for whatever reason, I don't feel I am the right person to help; I will refer them to a veterinary behaviorist for support. This is not to say that many clients dismiss this request; on the contrary, most are entirely on board when they understand the importance of absence suspension.

Understanding the gradual pace of training

I can't say enough about helping clients understand the gradual pace of separation anxiety training. Remember, the client does not typically have an intricate understanding of how desensitization works, and because of this, they need your help to have appropriate expectations for the pace of the protocol. In a discussion of the critical role of appropriate pacing of desensitization and counter-conditioning, Ballantyne notes: "These techniques may intensify the dog's fear and anxiety if used incorrectly" (2018). You and your client must understand that moving too quickly can backfire.

Without appropriate expectations, I can guarantee that a client will be more frustrated and get derailed from their training more quickly. You don't want a client to push their dog carelessly or go rogue with their protocol. Causing a dog to sensitize to absences by pushing too quickly is a dire mistake that we want to avoid at all costs.

There is a delicate balance between you as the trainer sounding like a Debbie Downer and you as the trainer setting realistic expectations. If you give the client any inkling of a time frame for successful resolution, they will either consciously or unconsciously expect that timeline and be discouraged if it approaches and they are still not at their goal.

Gentle reminders about the fact that the dog sets the pace will be valuable. Remember the empathy we discussed earlier in the book? Lean into that and let the client know that the efforts they are putting forth now are to ensure that their dog will no longer suffer in the future.

As an adjunct to understanding the pace of the protocol, the client must be on board with the fact that they are working with you to help the dog's overall welfare as opposed to merely eliminating the outward symptoms. Wanting the dog to no longer bark when alone is understandable, but there is so much more to it than that.

As a side note, you have to differentiate between what *you* feel is optimal for the dog versus what the client potentially wants. For instance, if you get the dog to the point that he is no longer barking, destroying things, or eliminating in the house, but he still looks a little uncomfortable, you may feel the need to continue working on the issue. But the client might be satisfied. I'm not going to lie, that can be really tough. Slowing down a protocol so that the dog is "perfect" can be a trainer error at times too. If the protocol is moving so slowly in hopes of achieving perfection, there is a possibility of losing the client, who just can't relate to your decision-making. I would never (ever!) suggest that you allow a dog to suffer, but if the client is content and the dog is doing well enough to be left alone without compromising welfare, that is a win you should consider taking.

Commitment to not using aversive tools or techniques

While I am adamant about not incorporating positive punishment into any type of training, I realize that average dog owners are not often aware of precisely what that means, nor do they have an understanding of the potentially dire fallout that can result. When working with a separation anxiety dog, it must be a priority that the client understands that their dog is experiencing fear, terror even.

I try to underscore the reasons that the use of punishment is so ineffective and also harmful when working with behavioral anxiety through using human examples. One such example has already been touched on in this book: the fear of flying. I have a dear friend who is terrified of flying, particularly during take-off. If during take-off, I were to yell at her or whack her upside the head and tell her to knock it off, I can guarantee that would not decrease her fear or make her future anxiety any better. If we repeated the initiation of punishment during every single take-off, her stress would likely increase because not only would she still be frightened of flying, but she would also be fearfully anticipating a blow to the head and angry yelling.

This is no different than what happens to our dogs when punishment is used during behavior modification. The range of disciplines I have seen implemented by clients includes everything from yelling to throwing chains to the use of shock collars. Each element on this punishment spectrum is not only useless in changing the anxiety feelings but is also detrimental to the dog's well-being.

We cannot fix fear with pain or intimidation.

You may be thinking about that *one* example of a dog who successfully stopped vocalizing when an electric collar was used. There is no question that pain or intimidation can sometimes suppress the outward manifestations of anxiety, but they are not able to relieve the anxiety itself. It may be an unpopular view for some trainers, but I vehemently believe that using punishment of any kind with a fearful dog is cruel and inhumane.

Going back to the client, their understanding of punishment is not always as in-depth as ours. It seems utterly logical to some clients that they would yell "No!" at their dog when he started barking or displaying other undesired behavior. The onus is entirely on us to educate our clients as to the inaccuracy of their reasoning.

Discussing the use of punishment should not be confrontational or reproachful. Dog owners are doing the best they can with what they know; there is nothing blameworthy about their misunderstanding of punishment and its effects.

Gently reviewing why the protocol has no inclusion of punishment methodologies is the way to proceed. Kindhearted explanations and examples are the appropriate focus for this conversation.

Approaching the punishment discussion in an inappropriate way can result in a client who feels guilt and may become alienated. There should be no blame in this conversation, only education.

So you are aware, I include a section in my client contract that states that the client has been informed that the use of aversive tools or punishment methodologies can result in dangerous behavior outcomes. Furthermore, a client's use of aversive tools or punishment methodologies as part of their separation anxiety protocol constitutes a breach of contract and will result in termination of services.

This section of the contract is simply for my protection and the protection of the dog, but of course, I gently discuss punishment before obtaining a signature.

The business side of separation anxiety

While the majority of this book is about the treatment process for separation anxiety, I think it is worth taking a moment to discuss the business side of things as well. Separation anxiety work can be done entirely remotely, and the benefits of doing so far outweigh working together in person, as you know.

Pricing your services

When working with separation anxiety, it is prudent to set up a pricing package that will span several weeks. Most CSATs start with a four-week package. I think this is important in that we know the dog will not progress all that quickly, and these first few weeks are generally foundation-building in nature. The four weeks will entail an initial assessment plus three additional reassessments. In addition to that, the client will be receiving their daily missions based on the feedback they provided in their notes the day prior.

It is common practice in our industry only to have the client pay for the live consult and then not pay for any additional communications, such as emails or phone calls. While I do think it is tricky to charge for every client interaction (that feels like nickel and diming), a package price that covers the approximate amount of time the trainer devotes to the client per week is entirely appropriate. It is wise to consider pricing in a way that will meet the trainer's needs for compensation, but also make the price reasonably affordable for the client. Remember, they may need several four-week packages to get through to the finish line.

When first working with separation anxiety, mission-writing is a slow process, but as you gain skill you will be able to write out daily missions rather quickly. I typically suggest that a trainer considers that they will be working about two-and-a-half to three hours a week for each separation anxiety client. If you were to take this number and multiply it by your typical hourly rate, that would give you a base package price. You can use that calculated price, or you can discount it a little due to the fact that all the work is being done remotely.

As training progresses with a client, and you get to know the dog and his humans better, your efficiency at mission-writing will improve. At the same time, you will be looking at larger quantities of data, and observing longer missions (as the dog's total alone-time tolerance increases). So, while you may be tempted to lower your price as the months move forward, I don't recommend that, as it has become all too obvious that the successive months are not any less work for the trainer.

Marketing

Marketing to those in need of separation anxiety services is important. However, there are many dog professionals out there who do not want to take on separation anxiety, so making your peers aware of your services is a great place to start in getting referrals. Because this service is remote and thereby you can take on clients anywhere in the world, it is important to have good SEO so that your services will be found in online searches. There is not nearly enough quality information available out there, so producing a blog or other materials that will help spread the word about your services, and give people hope as well, can be tremendously useful.

Scheduling

One of the lovely things about working with separation anxiety is that you can fit it in easily among your other client commitments. I set aside a few hours every morning to go through my clients' mission notes and write them new missions for the day. As long as you choose a similar time each day to write your missions, you and your client can get into an easy flow of knowing when the missions will be ready to do for the day.

Chapter 5
Implementing Behavior and
Training Plans

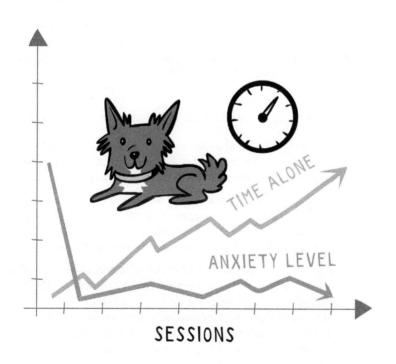

TIME ALONE

ANXIETY LEVEL

SESSIONS

In order to start working a behavior plan, we must do an initial assessment to briefly view the dog when alone. This will provide us the information needed to move forward in creating a day- to-day training plan.

Performing an initial assessment

The initial assessment, where we view the dog alone briefly, is conducted using live online viewing tools. Meeting live with the client and their dog allows you to gather preliminary knowledge about both the client's departure routines and the dog's body language when he is approaching threshold. It is also an opportunity for you and the client to discuss any concerns and review training protocol information and additional management strategies if needed.

We (the CSATs and I) do our initial assessments using Zoom to view the client and dog; however, as mentioned, there are numerous platforms available.

An initial assessment will take about an hour (occasionally a little more if the client has lots of questions). The portion of the assessment where you are watching the dog alone is rarely very long, typically only a few minutes. It is my goal for this to be the last time that the dog experiences an absence that is at or over threshold.

There are three things to consider when conducting the initial assessment.

1. If a client already has a video recording of their dog alone, you will likely not have to view the dog during an absence that is longer than comfortable since you will already have that data.

2. If the client has never left their dog alone for longer than he can handle, I strongly suggest that you not push the dog to the point of experiencing distress at all. This practice is not only unnecessary but also can be harmful to the dog.

3. If you are viewing a dog who is (for whatever reason) not displaying any signs of concern or anxiety during an absence, I suggest you still keep the entire duration of alone time at 30 minutes or less. Conduct a second assessment of a dog like this to confirm that you didn't get a false read or that the lack of worry observed was not an anomaly.

The only reason it is generally considered acceptable to push a dog slightly past his threshold in the initial assessment is that typically,

these dogs have been being left alone, and thus, we are not impos-
ing unaccustomed stress on the dog. Understand, though, that there
is no need to let a dog suffer in any way. Once you observe body
language that indicates the dog is starting to experience anxiety, the
assessment should end.

During the initial assessment, you can ask the client to go through their
entire leaving routine. This will help you in the future to identify various
pre-departure cues that may need to be incorporated in your protocol.
Observing the dog while the owner is getting ready allows you to see
whether those actions are triggers for the dog's concern or not.

Recording the initial assessment (easily done in Zoom) is a good
idea so that you not only have an inventory of the client's leaving
routine, you also have a baseline of the dog's body language that
can be carefully observed and compared to future sessions. As a side
note, we love using a small snippet of this first video in comparison
to a recording down the line to be able to clearly show the client
the dramatic change in the dog's behavior. This can be an excellent
motivational tool.

I often decide not to have the client watch the dog live during the
initial assessment. (It is, of course, up to the client if they really do
want to watch though.) Many clients are aware of their dog's separation anxiety but have never actually seen the dog during alone time;
they are only cognizant of the general behavior due to neighbor
complaints or evidence of destruction or elimination. It is not easy
to watch your beloved dog suffering, and if possible, I do try to spare
the client from witnessing the distressing behavior, particularly if
they are sensitive to it.

As a dog professional, it may even be hard for *you* to watch the upsetting behavior that the dog displays when alone. While no one should
be impervious, please keep two things in mind to help you:

1. This initial assessment is intended exclusively to gather
    information and should, therefore, be viewed as clinically
    as possible. It is not that I suggest you don't care or be con-
    cerned about the dog, but you are there to help change the
    outcome, and this is simply information that can help you
    implement that change.

2. This is the last time the dog will have to suffer in any way if
    you conduct your separation anxiety protocol gradually and

systematically. Have confidence in the knowledge that you are there to make a dramatic change not only for the life of that dog but also for the human who loves him.

Here are some important details about conducting an assessment:

You should start a timer the moment the exit door closes so you have an accurate timestamp of how long it takes for the dog to become anxious. The reason the timer initiates when the door closes is so you have a precise mechanism for future comparison. For instance, if you started the timer when the client was gathering her things, you would not be comparing apples to apples each time. Sometimes the client would take 30 seconds to get out the door, yet other times it might take 55 seconds of getting ready. You need a precise moment that the timer always begins. (Note: If you can hear the deadbolt, you can use the locking sound as the time to start the timer.)

When observing the dog, I suggest that you take quick, shorthand notes during the absence (and even during the departure routine if needed). My notes often reflect something like this:

0.00   Door closed

0.04   Dog approached the door

0.10   Dog sat

0.31   Dog pawed lightly at door

0.45   First small whine

1:13   Dog began pacing slightly around the room

2:02   Dog returned to the door and pawed at base

2:46   Dog started whining more

3:22   Two soft barks

3:26   Jumped at door

3:35   Client re-entered

3:40   Dog greets by jumping a few times

4:03   Dog heads to the couch and settles

While the above notes are written out for this example, each CSAT seems to have their own shorthand for behaviors. They may use abbreviations such as **S** for sit or **P** for pacing.

For those who use a mobile device as a timer, many have a "lap function" so that you can mark the times when behaviors occur. Don't worry about getting your notes perfect, particularly initially; you'll have a recording to refer to if needed.

Reporting findings to the client

Upon the client's return, allow the dog to settle a bit before you and the client regroup to discuss the absence and the next steps. Watching the dog's greeting behavior can be helpful for future comparison, as some dogs display excessive greeting when anxiety has occurred and are nonchalant when they have not experienced stress.

Talk to the client about what you have observed, but make sure that you relay observable, measurable behavior as opposed to your opinion about what the dog was feeling. This should always be the way you discuss the dog, whether in your own notes, in client communications, or exchanges with the veterinarian. An example of the correct versus the incorrect way to address the dog's behavior is as follows:

Incorrect:
Fluffy looked worried when you were walking toward the door with your keys, and then she started to really melt down after about 31 seconds. By three minutes she appeared upset and anxious and then she started barking.

Correct:
Fluffy was watching attentively while you were walking toward the door with your keys. At 4 seconds, she approached the door and remained standing until 10 seconds, when she sat. Fluffy gave one light paw at the exit door at 31 seconds and exhibited her first small whine at 45 seconds. At 1 minute and 4 seconds, Fluffy began mildly pacing. At 2 minutes, she returned to the door and lightly scratched at it with her paw. Fluffy began some faint whining at 2 minutes and 46 seconds, and by a little over 3 minutes she barked softly twice.

Hopefully, you can see the difference, not only between the subjective versus the objective content, but also how it might impact the client's feelings about the absence. The more objective style might even influence how *they* record their future notes.

Once you have reviewed the body language observations, you can spend time talking to the client about how you will proceed. This is an excellent time to lean into your client's empathy and make sure they understand the gradual pace that will be followed, particularly in this beginning stage.

The initial assessment is an excellent time to review the way you will be recording your client's mission each day and the requirements that you have for them as well. We do all of our missions in a Google Sheet, and we ask that the client enter their notes about the mission when they complete it. Similar to the example above, we want the client to record their notes using observable and measurable criteria. It is much more difficult for you if the client enters things in their notes that are subjective such as "Fluffy was freaked out," or even "Fluffy didn't seem worried." What do those statements actually mean in terms of the behavior? Was she barking, pawing, pacing, etc.? Or in the case of the second one, was she lying down with hip rolled to one side and head down? The last thing you want is for the client to give you notes like "She did fine." What does that mean exactly?

Preparing to begin training

We often create a sample mission with example notes for the client to refer to so that they understand how to write their notes. Some clients will follow your lead exactly; however, do know that many clients will need a little coaching to get it right.

I suggest that you let your client know you will be creating their mission at a particular time each day. For instance, I let my clients know that I write all missions between 6 and 8 a.m. so they know their new mission will be available by 8 a.m. Pacific Time. Additionally, the client knows that if their notes are not entered by 6 a.m. Pacific, they likely won't get a new mission for that day. It's rare for the client to miss a mission, but on occasion life gets in the way. In those circumstances, I simply enter a few notes to the client, letting them know that they can do yesterday's mission today instead of getting an entirely new mission.

One side note about this: If clients miss performing a mission, I do not let them accumulate their unrehearsed days as if they were unpaid time. The package is four consecutive weeks of missions, five days a week. If they get waylaid and can't get one done, that doesn't mean they get extra days at the end of their package. Yes, if they tell me in advance that they will be gone for a few days, I can adjust for that, but not merely for unplanned missed days.

The final component that you should keep in mind and tell your client about is that you can't know their dog intimately with just one assessment. It will take some rehearsals of absences and possibly a few reassessments to really have a full grasp on the dog's body language and individual threshold. That's fine, though. The full development of knowledge about the dog does not typically happen in Session 1 in any type of training.

Behavior plans

You have been extraordinarily patient in getting to this section and reading all of the lead-up information before this behavior plan segment. Bravissimo to you! If you cheated a tad and jumped ahead to this section, I get it, but please know that the other material is important, so please do not skip it altogether.

Behavior plans are the meat of what you, as the dog professional, will be doing with your client. The potatoes are equally important, though! Cheerleading and compassion round out a behavior plan and allow for the most effective results.

Training without a plan is a boo-boo that you should avoid.

While your mission criteria will adjust regularly and will be entirely based on the dog's performance, the overall plan for separation anxiety is a precise one. Refer back to the discussion on desensitizing dogs to being alone in the previous chapter if needed.

- Conduct about five days a week of gradual and systematic absence rehearsals that follow a particular set of rules.
- Stay beneath or at threshold at all times.
- Use warmups (discussed below) as needed with the individual dog (there are some exceptions).
    - Keep all warmups below 60 seconds (there are rare exceptions).

- ○ Use variability in your day-to-day criteria so as not to allow the dog to discern patterns (easy, medium, hard).
- Introduce pre-departure cues carefully and individually after some duration is achieved.
- Lower criteria in one aspect of difficulty if you are raising criteria in another aspect.
- Keep sessions at 20 to 30 minutes (there are some exceptions to this rule).
- Require the client to take mini-breaks between each step in their mission, approximately 30 to 90 seconds for each break on average.
- While the global goal of the missions is to increase alone time, make sure that you are incorporating easy wins for the dog on occasion to keep the foundation strong.
- The longest step in the mission is the final step (with variable warmups in advance).

We'll review the parts of the plan in further detail and look at a few example missions as well.

Conduct five days a week of absence rehearsals

The amount of time that a client devotes to their dog's separation anxiety protocol may vary, but in general, I recommend five days a week of absence rehearsals. Remember, these absence rehearsals (missions) are 20 to 30 minutes of time in their entirety. Within each mission are multiple steps where rehearsing small absences (coming and going) are incorporated.

I think it is important to mention here that I would far prefer a client devote fewer days to their training, as opposed to heaping on too much.

It seems logical that the more rehearsal devoted, the faster the protocol will work. Unfortunately, this is erroneous with separation anxiety training; too much time dedicated to absence rehearsals can be detrimental and cause sensitization. Proceed with caution.

You may have heard of the law of diminishing returns. This law is typically referred to when discussing economics, but it applies here as well. The input of additional units of time can result in decreased incremental return. For separation anxiety specifically, rehearsing more will not yield faster progress, and conversely, can create problematic outcomes.

So you know, the 20 to 30 minutes for training is not a particularly magical number. Years ago, I had clients devote more time to their training, yet I discovered two things in the process:

1. Many clients waned in their training efforts because the time required was too overwhelming to accomplish regularly.

2. It became apparent that more than 20 to 30 minutes of training did not yield much, if any, desensitization benefit. There's no sense in carrying out training that is low in returns, particularly when there is some risk involved.

When the dog has progressed to the point of 30 minutes or more of alone time, the total mission time will, of course, be longer than the early sessions that were 20 to 30 minutes in total. At this time in the protocol, it is sensible to have the client only conduct the longer absences two to three days a week. If they choose, they can still do short rehearsals on the other two or three days a week. This recommendation is, in part, about the client's ability to maintain training. Asking a dog owner to leave home for lengthy periods of time five days a week is unnecessary, and unreasonable for most clients anyway. Additionally, giving the dog those nice easy wins a few days a week can positively impact the training outcome.

A quick note about the two days off per week. I'm commonly asked whether those two days need to be split up or varied week to week. I suppose in an ideal world it would be good to split the days up and vary which days off were taken. In reality, though, the days off are often dictated by the client's schedule, and it doesn't seem to make a substantial difference, in most cases, if they fall on the same days, or if they are taken together. The purpose of taking days off is not only to give both the dog and the client a much-needed break, but also because we often see an increase in learning occur after rest periods. Often, after a little break from training, the dog appears to have "clicked," and makes more progress than if he had not received a training respite. This jump in learning is often described as "latent learning" (this is possibly an incorrect use of that phrase). This increase in learning after downtime is probably better labelled as "memory consolidation." For interesting reading on this topic, I highly recommend this blog post written by Eileen Anderson: https://eileenanddogs.com/blog/2016/12/19/latent-learning/.

Stay beneath or at threshold

You may be surprised that I mention both *beneath* threshold and *at* threshold here. I do this for two reasons.

Firstly, there will be times that, despite your best effort to avoid it, a dog may approach threshold unexpectedly. This is not necessarily because of an error on your part. It is merely the reality of working with a sentient being who may have varying factors that influence them on any given day. The threshold you choose should be carefully determined and should not be when the dog is experiencing full-blown anxiety, but rather when the dog is displaying body language that indicates stress is likely to develop. If you choose your threshold judiciously, you will stay beneath that full anxiety level most of the time.

The other reason that I mention "beneath or at" is that I feel it is erroneous to work far below threshold continually. While we should be steadfast about keeping the dog from experiencing distress, working at a level where the dog is so far under threshold that potential progress is dramatically reduced is flawed training for two reasons.

1. While it might seem as though going even more slowly will help the dog stay that much more comfortable, if you never approach the threshold you are hardly progressing, and improvement is diminished. Think about just tickling the underbelly of the dog's threshold as your aim for training.

2. We must also consider that the pace of the protocol needs to reflect forward progress to at least the point that the client can see (however subtly) that advancement is happening.

A personal human example might be helpful here. Let's say your goal is to run your first 5K. One trainer tells you to run a total of two minutes on your first practice (easy for you) and add 30 seconds at each practice. By your seventh practice, you are now running for five minutes, which would have been really hard for you the first day. A different coach tells you instead to run a total of 10 seconds on the first practice (super easy for you) and add 10 seconds each practice. By your seventh practice you are only running 70 seconds, which you could have easily done on the first day.

As the client with the goal of a 5K, you may feel that running five minutes consecutively right now is a bit of a challenge, but it is undoubtedly on the way toward accomplishing your goal after following the first trainer's guidelines. Conversely, when following the second trainer, you may feel discouraged by how far you (still) are from your ultimate goal. In reality, you might be right to feel that way. What have you accomplished in seven days with the second trainer that has allowed you to realize improvement? Little to nothing.

Hopefully, this depicts the importance of the balance that you must maintain. Being exaggeratedly conservative depletes some of the development of advancement and certainly can affect motivation.

To further this example, you might see how pushing too hard would be an error as well. Using our running analogy, if criteria are raised too fast, you would feel overtaxed and dispirited at your continued inability to maintain the requested pace. Your individual capacity is what should determine your training pace, just as the individual dog's ability should determine the pace of their separation anxiety protocol.

The last important point about threshold is this: Not only is it individual to that particular dog, it is also an always-moving target (or it should be).

If a dog begins their separation anxiety protocol by whining and barking at the four-second mark, as you move forward in the training, that threshold will move. In time, after working on the protocol a bit, you might see that the dog no longer whines at the first four seconds, but instead, begins to show subtle signs of vigilance and is potentially getting ready to whine at the 20-second mark or more. The duration of the threshold and the way the dog displays it need to be watched persistently as the dog makes progress.

Using warmups

The concept of warmups is important for creating missions. While not all dogs benefit from multiple warmups, the majority do, at least in the beginning of a protocol. Our goal is to get the dog feeling very ho-hum about the comings and goings that are happening. Warmups allow for this.

I'd like you to think of warmups as the National Anthem before the ball game. The warmups (like the anthem) are signifiers that the game is about to begin.

Let's say the dog reaches threshold around five minutes of being left alone. Rather than simply repeat multiple repetitions of five-minute absences, we can use warmups to achieve that five minutes more easily. Warmups allow for increased efficiency and will help preclude potential sensitization.

An example of a mission for a dog whose threshold was five minutes might be as follows:

Note: To be clear, this is a mission for one particular dog that may or may not be at all appropriate for any other given dog. It is solely reflective of this specific dog's current capability at the time it was written.

Mission Example for Fluffy (with sample notes)

Set up laptop and gate - go hang out and relax for about 5 minutes before beginning

Exit the gate, exit the door, wait 2 seconds, return
Fluffy walked with me to the gate and remained standing quietly during the absence

Exit the gate, exit the door, lock deadbolt, immediately return
She remained on the couch but lifted her head when the deadbolt was locked

Exit the gate, exit the door, lock deadbolt, wait 10 seconds, return
Fluffy lifted her head when the deadbolt locked and left the couch at 8 seconds

Exit the gate, exit the door, wait 5 seconds, return
She remained on the couch the entire time with her head down

Exit the gate, exit the door, lock deadbolt, wait 10 seconds, return
She lifted her head with the deadbolt but remained lying down for the duration

Exit the gate, exit the door, wait 3 seconds, return
She didn't lift her head and remained lying on the couch

Exit the gate, exit the door, lock deadbolt, immediately return
She didn't lift her head at the deadbolt this time, yay!

Exit the gate, exit the door, lock deadbolt, and return at exactly 30 seconds

(begin timing when you lock the deadbolt, end timing when you open the door)
Fluffy didn't lift her head at the deadbolt but did so at the 17 second mark. Remained on the couch until 25 seconds and then walked slowly to the gate. Returned to lying down when I walked in.

Notice that there are multiple steps in the overall mission, and the first seven steps while varying in difficulty are all relatively easy respective to the final absence step. These steps represent the warmups. By the time the dog has watched you exit and return several times, they know that the "game" is happening. Imagine the dog thinking, "This is that *thing* Mom does where she goes in and out a bunch of times. It's no big deal."

Hopefully you understand the idea of the warmups initiating the game, but I suspect you might be thinking, "Why not do several repetitions of absences nearer to the dog's threshold during the mission? You said not to do too much work way below threshold!" Excellent – you're thinking on your toes!

Approaching or hitting threshold once is sufficient for the day's rehearsal. Similar to a trigger stacking example that you might use with a reactive dog, if you were to approach threshold multiple times in a training session, the cumulative effect could itself cause a dog to go over threshold.

Imagine working with a dog who is reactive on leash toward passing dogs. You are sitting on a park bench counter-conditioning the dog. As planned, some stranger dogs pass in the distance. But several times during your session there are dogs whose distance from you approaches the dog's threshold – can you see how the snowballing effect might impact the dog? If a few dogs came a bit close, you would counter-condition and then likely call it a day. A successful ending for all. This is the same notion that we are using with separation anxiety missions.

If you are still using your critical thinking cap right now, you might also be wondering if these warmups would lead to a dog who differentiates between the real absences and those that have warmups... kudos for your advanced reasoning!

Initially, we use warmups to help the dog be comfortable through repetition, but as a protocol progresses, we can slowly decrease the warmups (variably) so they become fewer and fewer. Think of decreasing warmups as similar to a wean-off process. Eventually, walking out the door for the very first time is no different than walking out the tenth time. When we arrive at that point, we typically call the absence a "one-and-done," meaning that we no longer need any warmups and we can simply leave. The mere appearance of you walking out the door signifies that an unexciting event is about to occur.

Isn't conditioning awesome?

Depending on the duration that the dog can be comfortable with alone time, I suggest that warmups be no longer than 60 seconds. Even when the dog can be successfully alone for 12 minutes (or more), you will keep all of the individual warmups under one minute.

The objective of the warmups is to not only initiate the game but also to be easy for the dog to accomplish.

Remember, missions will be made up of several steps that result in a total duration of training time of about 20 to 30 minutes. In the early stages, you may have multiple warmups, but you will continually be evaluating and discerning how few warmups might be needed as the dog progresses. Make sure not to decrease warmups in a straight line and also be certain not to conduct the same warmup each time.

Today's mission might have six warmups that begin where the first one is the client exiting the door for three seconds and then returning. Tomorrow's mission might have seven warmups where the first one is the client exiting the door for one second and returning. The following day may only have five warmups where the first one is the client exiting the door for five seconds and returning.

You can see that we are varying both the *number* and *difficulty* of all the steps within a mission. (Remember to randomize between easy, medium, and hard.) The process of scattering or fluctuating the number and difficulty of the steps in a mission will keep the dog from discerning any patterns. Avoiding the formation of discernible patterns in all aspects of separation anxiety training is essential.

Incorporating predictability

Some materials suggest that one way to treat separation anxiety is to uphold a strict routine so that the dog knows exactly what is about to occur. In essence, this suggestion is stating that the dog's life should be predictable. There is some merit to considering the idea of predictability, but not necessarily with respect to stringent routines.

We are using predictability in the separation anxiety training recommended in this book. The predictability factor is that absences predict safety through gradual desensitization. In essence, we are incrementally generalizing *all* absence to reliably predict safety.

The concern I have with establishing a concrete routine for the dog instead of generalizing absence safety is that it is hard, if not impossible, for the client to maintain. There will inevitably be times when the client has to rush out the door and will not be able to uphold the exact routine that was established. Teaching the dog that *any* type of absence is safe is much more easily sustainable for all.

Pre-departure cues

We've talked a little about pre-departure cues or triggers, as we often call them, but now we'll go into a bit more depth.

A trigger is anything that might indicate to the dog that an absence will occur. Typically discussed triggers are things like putting on shoes or a coat or picking up the keys.

You should be very mindful that not all triggers occur *before* exiting the door. (Hence the word trigger makes a little more sense than pre-departure cue.) If the client exits the door and then audibly walks down a gravel path to an exterior gate that creaks on its hinges, you can assume that those noise elements might be triggers as well. Hearing (and even smelling) the owner can constitute departure cues.

Instead of spending time trying to uncouple these departure cues from the absence, the most efficient way to train is to realize that these triggers will continue to be prompts that an absence is occurring. Remember, the dog will always be aware that you are going to leave after such activities as gathering your bag and keys. Rather than try and teach him that these *don't* signify an absence, it is much preferred to incorporate those cues instead so that they still lead to absences, but the absences themselves are not scary. The stimuli of keys and bag remain predictors, but they now predict something safe (an under-threshold absence).

Here is an example of a mission with the pre-departure of keys included:

Mission Example for Buddy (with pre-departure cue of keys)

Set up laptop and gate - go hang out and relax for about 5 minutes before beginning

Walk to the door and **pick up your keys**, wait 2 seconds and return

Walk to the door and **pick up your keys**, open and close the door immediately, return

Walk to the door and **pick up your keys**, wait 2 seconds and return

Walk to the door and **pick up your keys**, wait 2 seconds and return

Walk to the door, open and exit for 5 seconds with door closed, return (no keys)

Walk to the door and **pick up your keys**, exit and close the door for 1 second, return

Walk to the door and **pick up your keys**, exit and close the door for 5 seconds, return

Walk to the door and **pick up your keys**, replace keys immediately and return

Walk to the door, open and exit for 3 seconds with door closed, return (no keys)

Walk to the door and **pick up your keys**, replace keys immediately and return

Walk to the door, open and exit for 20 seconds with door closed, return (no keys)

Setting criteria

Remember, it is critical to lower criteria in one aspect of difficulty if you are raising criteria in another aspect. This is true whether we are discussing departure cues or other challenges – when increasing the difficulty of one element of an exercise, you will typically lower another aspect of that exercise.

You can see in the example mission above that when the keys were integrated, the duration in those individual steps was lowered.

Another example of shifting criteria might be to lower the difficulty of the step but increase duration. Remember, every time a dog is at home alone successfully, they are learning that alone time is safe. So, for this example we might increase the duration that the owner is gone but have them simply walk away from the home instead of driving the car away. Pulling the car out tends to be a salient cue to the dog, so removing the car from the equation makes this step easier, which allows us to increase duration.

Think about all of the details that can influence an absence to make it harder or easier when incorporated or removed. Keys tend to be a big one, and deadbolting the door is another. Driving the car away from the home might have to be broken down, and even incorporating the ding of the elevator in an apartment building can be considered a cue. Try to toggle these types of triggers in and out in a randomized way so that you can build duration with their incorporation more easily.

Session length

You've read this numerous times by now, but it bears repeating: *Keep sessions at 20 to 30 minutes.* When creating missions for your client, the number of steps included should cumulatively result in 20 to 30 minutes of training. Imagine if you had 20 steps in a mission with approximately 60 seconds of a break between each one – that would be 20 minutes just for the breaks and then you'd have to add in the time spent executing the steps as well. That would be way too much.

Missions that take 20 to 30 minutes are the norm, but there are a few important exceptions.

1. Puppies, and sometimes geriatric dogs, are candidates for shorter sessions. Typically, 10- to 15-minute sessions are sufficient. If they are that short and the dog is handling them well, conducting two sessions a day (on average, but be variable) during the five days a week is fine. This would mean that collectively, there would still be about 20 to 30 minutes in a day; it would simply be broken up. We know the needs of puppies and sometimes geriatrics can require shorter increments of training in many training categories; separation anxiety is no different.

2. There are some outlier dogs for whom warmups are not helpful. In fact, on occasion, a dog will actually start to show signs of increasing concern with successive warmups as opposed to the increase in calm behavior that we most often see. It is readily apparent after a few training sessions when

we come across this type of dog. In this situation, I recommend that the client has a handful of randomized absences to perform throughout the day. An example might be five absences to do at various times in a day, but none of them would contain warmups.

Mini-breaks

Require the client to take mini-breaks between each step in their mission (approximately 30 to 90 seconds for each break on average).

Why? you ask.

Have you ever thought about how many cold trials you get in any given training session? Whether you are training a sit or working on behavior modification, you get one cold trial in any given training session. One.

Let's look at an example using a different type of behavior modification – training for object resource guarding. When you begin your training session with a resource guarding dog, you are going to conduct a succession of exchanges with objects. You'd begin with a non-guarded object if conducting an appropriate protocol, which, if you think about it, is another great example of how we use warmups in training.

You give the dog the object and step away. When you return to approach the dog, you will be giving a treat after removing the non-guarded object. That was your one cold trial, right there. (You could even argue that this isn't a categorical cold trial because you did a training "set-up," but let's not get too picky for the purposes of this example.) Once you return the object to start your second repetition, the dog is fully aware of the game you are playing, so none of your successive exchanges would be consider cold trials.

This is exactly the same with separation anxiety training sessions. Since we get one and only one cold trial, our job is to make each successive trial as much like a cold trial as possible. Taking breaks between steps is the way to accomplish this. Again, I recommend that breaks be no shorter than 30 seconds, but 90 seconds is typically sufficient. There are definitely outliers in this aspect of the protocol as well, so for occasional dogs a longer break is preferred between steps.

Two additional important characteristics of taking breaks are as follows:

1. You absolutely must vary the duration of the breaks that the client is taking between steps. If your client is savvy you can just tell them to vary the length of time. If they need a bit more instruction to keep on track, you can give them specified yet varying break times to follow.

2. The sole purpose of these breaks is to make the succeeding steps as much like a cold trial as possible. One error that I see made continually by owners and trainers alike is waiting for the dog to completely settle on the breaks. Let's look at that for a moment.

You do one step (say exit the door for 10 seconds) and then return. Fluffy has gotten up off her bed during the absence, but is not at all displaying anxiety. You take your break. While taking your break you wait until Fluffy has returned to her bed. You are watching her and waiting until she completely settles and rests her head. When that occurs, you get up to begin your next step. Can you see the potential for something undesirable to be learned here? Remember, dogs are masters of discrimination, right? So, if each time you take a break, you wait for Fluffy to be on her bed resting her head down, she will conceivably learn that the act of placing her head down leads to you leaving – no more head-down behavior from Fluffy! Again, the breaks are merely to help establish the next step to be as much like a cold trial as possible. The breaks are not intended to be used as a time for the dog to settle into a particular position.

Mission duration: easy wins, randomness, and timing of long departures

While the global goal of the overall missions is to increase alone time, make sure that you are *incorporating easy wins for the dog* on occasion to keep the foundation strong. This means that you will not increase the difficulty of your steps every single day. This is incredibly important whether you are looking at the warmups or the final step. Easy wins are critical.

Your variability between easy, medium, and hard is important, but *be extremely cautious about creating any sort of pattern,* whether within a specific day, or over the course of a week or more. The message we are trying to give the dog is that any absence is safe, not that absences will always occur in predictable ways. Human beings are terrible at randomization so make sure you are watching your steps carefully and avoid creating any patterns. An example of a pattern that we often see is this: One day the mission is hard, the next day it's easy, and the third day it is medium/moderate. Then on day four that pattern repeats itself. You can see how the dog, in time, might discern the overall pattern. Some dogs do so really quickly too!

Finally, remember that *the most difficult step in the mission is the final step* (with variable warmups in advance). The early steps in the mission are warmups, which establish that the game is being played. These variable steps lead up to the final step (sometimes called the terminal step), which will be the most difficult in the series. This final step in the mission is the one that will come closest to the dog's threshold and, as such, we can end after we complete that. As we progress to being able to leave the dog alone for appreciable durations, we will no longer need warmups, but simply do the longest duration, so this is in preparation for that. When you get to the point of dropping all warmups, we call it a "one and done."

Your terminal step is the one that tickles that underbelly of threshold; it is the most challenging in the mission. Also, be aware that the difficulty of a step might not always be about duration. Stepping out the door for a shorter duration but walking audibly down the gravel path instead of remaining just outside the door would be one example of a challenging parameter for a final step in a mission.

The reason that we conduct the final step as the most challenging is for reasons of efficiency. The warmups are essentially cues to settle. They are easy steps that are under one minute in duration, and they allow for considerable opportunity to quickly go through and incorporate all the different variables, of which there are many. As we work toward having no warmups and doing a one and done, the only step in the mission will be the most difficult one. Since we approach threshold in the final step, there is no reason to continue doing easy steps after that is completed. It likely wouldn't hurt anything, but there is a chance that we could start to sensitize the dog if we put him in a situation where we were trigger stacking (creating additional stressors, even very easy ones, after an absence that came close to the dog's threshold tolerance). There are definitely diminishing returns to doing desensitization all day long; 20 to 30 minutes five days a week is an efficient and effective means to working with separation anxiety.

Three elements of successful duration changes

1. Incorporate easy wins.

2. Randomize the changes in duration.

3. Make sure the final step of the mission is the longest.

Chapter 6
Medication and Alternative Remedies

Before we go through some of the standard pharmacological and alternative therapies that can be used to treat separation anxiety, I want to clearly state my personal experiences so that you, my reader, can review the information presented here with full knowledge of the potential influence that my beliefs may contribute. In the past 20 years of working with separation anxiety, I have developed a firm pro-pharmacology bias due to countless positive experiences I have observed with my clients and their dogs. I used to feel more enthusiastic about the use of alternative remedies, but that feeling has waned over time due to various experiences. I suggest that you do your own research. Some works, all listed in the Reference section in the back of the book, worth checking out include Appleby and Pluijmakers (2004), Cannas et al. (2014), Sherman and Mills (2008), and Ballantyne (2018).

The topic of medication use for behavioral concerns is rife with conflict between numerous strong beliefs and researched facts. The only other issue that comes to mind that is equally controversial is canine nutrition; both topics are hornet's nests and have heavy bias on both sides.

Some understanding of medication and its role in separation anxiety is important. Why? Because our clients are being bombarded with information from every direction. While it's not the job of a non-veterinarian to advise or counsel about medication for any reason, it is undoubtedly useful for dog professionals to be aware of what the client is considering and how it may or may not affect the overall training and welfare of the dog.

As a side note, dog trainers who are working closely (day to day) with owners and their dogs are ideal sources of information for the veterinarian, with the client's approval of course. Through remote observations, in addition to data tracking, non-veterinary dog professionals can often discern emerging patterns in the dog's behavior. Discussing these observations with the client and the vet can aid in their determination of the right administration of medications.

Medications, alternative remedies, and budgets
Owners of separation anxiety dogs have an individually limited bandwidth of time, finances, and emotions to devote to helping their dogs. I have concluded that the protection of these "bandwidth resources" is of vital importance. Any training process or product inclusion that chips away at those resources without some positive influence on the training outcome has become a concern to me.

When clients devote time, money, and emotions to the process without benefit, we can draw nearer to the end of the resource pool without getting closer to a resolution, and I feel that is dangerous in many cases. Morally and ethically, I think it is my job to make sure the client can best help their dog within the amount of time or the budget that they have available.

I have many persuasive examples that influenced me over the years concerning medication use. The following story is just one example that helped turn the tide for me.

A previous client I worked with, Allie, had a dog named Polly with multiple behavior issues. Those issues, which included separation anxiety, were not only wreaking havoc on Allie's life, but also on the welfare of all the dogs in the household. Allie was adamant about not using pharmacology. She herself used only holistic remedies for her ailments – no ibuprofen for headaches or Nyquil for cold symptoms in this gal's bathroom drawers.

As our training continued forward, Allie decided that she was willing to try some natural remedies in hopes of realizing further progress – progress that was virtually nonexistent at the time. Fortunately, unlike many clients, Allie did choose to consult with a holistic veterinarian about how to proceed. (Many clients just research and purchase natural products on the internet, a practice we will discuss shortly.)

Allie's veterinarian was well-versed in alternative remedies and from the start, various natural products were used in combination. The vet aptly required the slow integration of these remedies in addition to careful monitoring how Polly's behavior was influenced. After the first round of treatments was tried and shown to be ineffective, a new set of products was introduced, and the next observation period began. It was typically a few weeks to a few months before each mixture was tried and then discarded as either not at all helpful, too laden with side effects, or at best, only minimally useful in affecting behavior. The cycle of trying something new, waiting for results, removing one preparation, and starting yet another dragged on and on. About a year into training combined with uncounted alternative therapies, Allie was not only discouraged and exasperated but financially depleted and feeling helpless.

At this point, the veterinarian who had been supportive of Allie's desire to only use holistic preparations began to advise the use of pharmaco-logic agents. It took some time, but finally, in her desperation, Allie agreed to try medication. Polly was given a common antidepressant remedy. Within about a month, not only was Polly responding beautifully and making tremendous strides in her training, but the entire household of resident dogs was noticeably improved. Allie had known that Polly was affecting her other dogs, but the changes in the home were even more profound than she imagined.

It is logical for you to think that this story is simply an argument that the medications worked better than the alternative remedies, and that conclusion wouldn't be entirely off point. However, this story did more for me than just instilling a strong belief in meds.

A few months after the onset of positive changes for Polly and her housemates, Allie and I were on a call, and to my utter surprise, she was crying and sounded miserable. I was there for her in every way, and thus ready to discuss what was happening. I expected to hear that some sort of regression had occurred, but her tears weren't about any such thing.

Allie poured her soul out to me exclaiming that she suddenly realized that she had subjected not just Polly to a diminished quality of life, but her other dogs as well, never mind the challenges that the human par-ticipants surrounding her had endured. Her guilt was crushing, and my heart broke for her as I listened through her endless tears. Regret is a terrible thing, and while it is not useful to look back and foster guilt over obviously positive intentions, I could understand the feelings that Allie was experiencing. In Allie's case, we were able to talk through the emotions and come out the other end with profound relief for the progress in Polly and the other dogs. A happy ending for all.

I couldn't help but think at that time, though, what if Allie hadn't had the same amount of money to allocate, time to devote, or emo-tional strength to bestow? In other circumstances where resources were more limited, might a client have given up long before?

As a result of Allie's experience and that of so many others, I have arrived at a belief that many of the alternative remedies that typically fall into the "Can't Hurt, Might Help" category, really actually *could* be considered unfavorable if they consume resources without provid-ing benefit.

Therein lies the basis for the bias that I have.

Do understand though, I have revealed my *bias* for the sake of transparency, but I am not in any way implying that biases are a bad thing! We *all* have them. Biases are merely mental shortcuts that allow us to reach decisions quickly.

Please do me a favor and take a moment to recognize whatever bias you may have (which might be very different than mine), so that when you review this section on medication, you can acknowledge the lens you are looking through.

Oh, and lastly, I want you to know that I wholeheartedly respect and appreciate all the different biases and those individuals who hold them, particularly those of my clients!

Behavioral pharmacology
I'll start this section with a brief discussion of the available pharmacology and then discuss a few alternative remedies as well. Keep in mind that this information is current at the time of publication, but much can and does change in the world of therapeutic research, so the data could already be out of date by the time you read this book. What is known is that there is usually a role for medications but that they need to be used in associated with behavior modification. Suzanne Hetts states that "No medication has been shown to be effective in reducing separation anxiety without concurrent behavior modification" (2012). Karen Overall goes so far as to argue that "Separation anxiety is an emergency. It should never be treated without medications once clinical signs are apparent" (Green, 2014).

An important note: Medications for anxiety-related conditions fall into two general types, maintenance and situational medications.

Maintenance medications
While the word maintenance seems to imply that we are sustaining a behavior, what the term means here is that the medications are used as daily support. There are two FDA-approved and widely used maintenance medications for separation anxiety in the United States: **Reconcile** and **Clomicalm**.

The things your clients need to know about these two commonly prescribed separation anxiety medications include:

- They are not habit forming.

- They are not sedatives.

- They are not new; they are heavily researched and are safe to use.

- They won't change a dog's personality except to reduce overall anxiety, which may mean the dog becomes even more fabulous than he already is.

- They will likely not have to be permanent (many dogs can be weaned off or put on a reduced dose once the problem has been resolved).

- They aren't prescribed because an owner is lazy and doesn't want to do the work. On the contrary, they support a proper treatment protocol.

Reconcile and Clomicalm both fall into the "antidepressant" classification and are administered as daily support as opposed to episodically. (We'll talk about situational meds shortly.)

The generic version of Reconcile is fluoxetine, which is almost universally known as Prozac. Reconcile is a selective serotonin reuptake inhibitor (SSRI), and this classification of medication has been heavily researched.

One thing that has impressed me with the brand of Reconcile is how they present their information. They do not make grandiose or false claims at all and are clear about the fact that the medication is an adjunct to training, not a stand-alone therapeutic agent.

Several quotes from the Reconcile website make me pleased, such as the following:

> *Your dog is not bad or spiteful, but is suffering from a readily treatable condition.*

> *When it is clear that the behaviors are not caused by a physical problem, your veterinarian will develop a comprehensive treatment plan for separation anxiety that may involve medication, behavior training and owner commitment. Reconcile® chewable tablets, when administered in conjunction*

with a simple training plan that you undertake at home, is one treatment option that has been shown to reduce these problematic behaviors.

Behavior modification training is an essential component in the treatment of separation anxiety in dogs.

Inappropriate use of Reconcile chewable tablets without concurrent behavior modification may not provide any lasting benefit of therapy.

A note about serotonin

While most non-veterinary dog professionals don't need to know the mechanism by which Reconcile or other medications work, I actually think it's fascinating and useful, so I will take a moment to explain it (albeit maybe a bit crudely).

The brain has a variety of neurotransmitters whose job it is to relay numerous types of information; one of these neurotransmitters is serotonin. Neurotransmitters are essentially chemical messengers (think itsy-bitsy bike messengers here) that transmit a signal. The component of the chemical process that I consider critical for us to know is that the neurotransmitter serotonin already exists in the brain *naturally*. The public generally associates serotonin with contributing to feelings of happiness and well-being; however, its actual biological function is a bit more complicated than that. Its job includes things like modulation of cognition, reward, learning, memory, and several physiological processes.

Appropriate levels of serotonin are shown to contribute to the reduction of anxiety and other mood stabilization actions. The job of fluoxetine is to allow serotonin to be adequately absorbed to maintain this higher level. Essentially, this medication is merely fostering a function that already exists in the brain. The reason I believe this knowledge can be valuable to understand is that it helps individuals realize that this medication's job is not to "dope up" a dog or cause unwanted sedation; it is merely promoting optimal serotonin levels. The newer SSRIs (like fluoxetine) have fewer side effects and fewer interactions with other drugs.

I've heard talk of concerns about one potential side effect: serotonin syndrome. This can occur if extremely high levels of serotonin exist; however, the research shows that it is nearly impossible to reach overdose levels with suitably administered levels of a single antidepressant drug. This condition is rarely seen and would typically require a combination of serotonin medications to achieve.

Many of our clients' dogs have benefited significantly from the use of this medication. From an observational standpoint, side effects have been minimal. The most common reported side effects (which match our clients' observations) seem to be inappetence and drowsiness, both of which appear to occur only in the beginning stages for most dogs taking the medication.

One of the veterinarians that I have worked with closely once told me that she meticulously advises her clients that, if this or any behavior medication is causing side effects that change a dog's personality or diminish positive attributes, then it is likely either the wrong dose or the wrong med for that individual. I loved hearing that, because I feel it is so vital for individuals to know that these medications are intended to better the animal's life overall – there is no need to diminish a dog's already jovial characteristics or create a doped dog.

Clomicalm is the other approved and widely used medication for separation anxiety. Its generic version is clomipramine, which is less familiar to the public. Clomipramine is a human-trialed medication that has been around since the 1960s. It is a tricyclic antidepressant, and instead of only acting on the neurotransmitter serotonin, it also influences another neurotransmitter called norepinephrine. Like Reconcile, the chemical processes involved serve to help optimize the levels of brain chemicals that are already present.

Many of our clients' dogs have also benefited from the use of this medication, and from what we have observed, drowsiness is the most common side effect, although the slightly less common inappetence can also be present. Both of those side effects also appear to be transient.

Whether any given dog is going to be positively influenced by either of these medications is specific to the individual. Some dogs do great on one and not the other and vice versa. Some veterinarians prefer to start with one of these or potentially even other medications that are considered off label. Off label (or extra-label) means that the drug is not approved for that particular clinical condition, which in this case is separation anxiety in dogs. They may be approved for other fear or anxiety-type behaviors, so their potential benefit is not without merit; it's just not yet approved for this specific condition.

The choice of medication used for any dog is entirely up to the veterinarian, so none of the information presented here is intended to promote or dissuade the use of any particular remedy. Furthermore, I want everyone to be aware that any substance that will be administered to a dog, even those that are considered natural and are available over the counter, should be reviewed and authorized by a veterinarian.

Episodic (situational) medication
Various medications can be used episodically for a sedating or calming effect that lasts only for a handful of hours. These are typically used during times when the dog is going to be alone (not prematurely alone if you are following the desensitization protocol in this book). The typical class of pharmacology used in this category is called benzodiazepines, but there are others outside of this class as well.

Benzodiazepines are in a family of drugs commonly known as minor tranquilizers. These meds act in a way that is sleep-inducing and anxiolytic (anti-anxiety). Benzodiazepines are categorized into one of three groups based on the amount of time it takes the body to eliminate half of the dose (this is called the half life). There are long-acting, short-acting and intermediate-acting compounds. The veterinarian will choose the appropriate compound for any individual dog.

Understandably, these meds can cause sedation. It also should be understood that a paradoxical reaction can occur, which means the individual would be more rather than less agitated. Because of the possibility of a dog having a paradoxical reaction to these meds, it is highly suggested by veterinarians that the medication is first trialed during a time when the owner is home so the client can observe the dog's behavior to ensure it is working appropriately for its desired effect.

Most of the benzodiazepines also act as appetite stimulants, which can be desirable for those dogs whose anxiety results in appetite loss. Benzodiazepines are controlled substances in the United States because they are frequently misused for recreation and can be abused. There is concern about the use (and particularly misuse) of benzodiazepines as they can be habit-forming.

There are a few other medications that have become more popular to use in the last decade for situational use. **Trazodone** is a med which has achieved considerable popularity for anti-anxiety use. It can be prescribed either for episodic or daily use. While trazodone is an antidepressant medication that works by inhibiting the reuptake of serotonin, norepinephrine, and dopamine, it also possesses sedating properties and therefore has become an alternative to benzodiazepine use for some veterinarians when dealing with anxious behaviors. Unlike benzodiazepines, trazodone is not a controlled substance, and while it does not have the same habit-forming properties, it can cause problems if taken continually and then discontinued abruptly, which is a trait common to many antidepressants.

Because trazodone has been much more commonly prescribed in the past ten years, we have observed numerous dogs for whom it was prescribed. Many of these dogs have received a positive benefit. Others have not exhibited much change in behavior during its use. As with any drug used for behavior, individual dogs respond differently.

There are two other medications that we have seen used episodically (though sometimes daily) and appear to be more common now than just a handful of years ago. The first is clonidine. **Clonidine** started to gain popularity in its use for fear-based behaviors after information was presented at a veterinary symposium in 2010. In 2011 the esteemed Dr. Nicholas Dodman released a study with Dr. Niwako Ogata in the *Journal of Veterinary Behavior* called "The use of clonidine in the treatment of fear-based behavior problems in dogs: An open trial." This study suggests that clonidine may not only be useful but also well-tolerated for the treatment of fear-based behavior problems in dogs. Since that time, we have seen more use of this medication with dogs who are suffering from separation anxiety.

Clonidine is a medication typically used to treat high blood pressure; however, behavior applications are not uncommon. Clonidine works by slowing the pulse rate, which is one of the mechanisms that can reduce anxiety. Clonidine is also a mild sedative. While veterinarians seem to prescribe it less often than trazodone for anxiety use, we have been able to observe numerous clients for whom it has been prescribed. It has appeared to be effective with some dogs, while others show little to no response. This points to the argument that persistence is valuable for owners when working with a vet in their efforts to find the right medication for their dog.

The last medication to bring up that has also been realizing some popularity for use with separation anxiety is gabapentin. **Gabapentin** has been used off label for the treatment of anxiety disorders. There is some debate over whether evidence is sufficient to support its use for this purpose. Gabapentin is an anticonvulsant medication used primarily to treat human partial seizures and neuropathic pain. We have observed a fair number of client dogs who have been prescribed this medication, and the results are varied, ranging from valuable benefit to no advantage at all. Be aware that there are no studies that evaluate the use of gabapentin to alter behavior in dogs.

While there are numerous other medications in both the daily and episodic classes that have been used for separation anxiety, the ones listed here are currently those that we observed as the most widely used.

In a recent publication by Leslie Sinn, DVM (2018), the following key points were made about the three medications mentioned above.

- Recent findings focusing on such drugs as trazodone, clonidine, and gabapentin have revolutionized how clinicians handle and treat dogs and cats.
- The results of these studies should be applied in the clinical setting with caution and with a full understanding of the potential pros and cons of using these medications.
- Despite promising results, additional research is desperately needed regarding pharmacokinetics, frequent and infrequent side effects, long-term behavioral impact, and the most clinically appropriate and effective use of these drugs.

Client resistance to medications

Some clients resist the very notion of using medication. To be able to discuss these concerns with your client, you need a basic understanding of the medications used for separation anxiety, which I've provided above. Next, let's take a look at some of the most common apprehensions people have about using medications to treat their dog's anxiety and hopefully assuage any concerns:

It's merely sedation, will change the dog's personality, or will have undesirable side effects. The medications that are typically used for separation anxiety are not sedatives. While some veterinarians might prescribe a sedative for episodic purposes, that is not the kind of medication we are usually referring to. For separation anxiety, a veterinarian will most commonly prescribe an antidepressant, which is designed to help mitigate the anxiety that the dog is experiencing, rather than simply sedate the dog.

With antidepressants, drowsiness or lethargy are not commonly seen, except possibly as an early side effect, which tends to go away fairly quickly. What we usually do see, instead, is a more happy-go-lucky dog, because the medication is doing its job to lower anxiety. Large personality changes aren't something that we observe often, and that is certainly not the goal. But if they do happen, a change is appropriate, and there are other medications to try.

The risk of serious side effects is rather rare, but as with any type of medication, monitoring the dog is important in the event that a change may be needed. Possible side effects with most of the commonly prescribed SA medications can vary, and as such, keeping a watchful eye as to how the dog is reacting is important. Veterinarians will typically be appropriately cautious by monitoring the dog in many ways, including blood tests.

Using medication makes the owner feel like a failure, and raises concerns about being judged. I wish I could shout from the mountaintops that you are not failing your dog by using medication. You are helping your dog! Beings experiencing anxiety are suffering. Studies have shown that when medication is used in tandem with separation anxiety training, the pace of the training goes faster. Also, making a choice to use medication does not mean that the dog's condition is therefore deemed severe. In actuality, anxiety doesn't have to be entirely debilitating for meds to be beneficial.

I realize that judging *people* for their behavioral-pharma use is still pervasive in our culture. Hence, it's not a big leap that some may likewise judge us for giving medication to our dogs. When doing what is best for your dog, whatever that may be, feel strong in your decision. What's best for you, your family, and your dog is what really matters.

The dog should be able to get better with training alone. Well, this might be true is some cases, but it also might not. Let's look at from a different perspective. If your best friend was suffering from extreme depression – she's unable to work, she's not eating, she's crying nonstop – and you knew that she could begin feeling better much faster if she took medication while undergoing therapy, would you want her to wait a few months to see if the therapy could get the job done on its own? I've seen so many dogs feel better sooner and overcome their separation anxiety much faster with medications, so when I discovered that my Tini had separation anxiety, I worked with my vet to find the right medication for her while I trained her.

Medication is unnatural. Any substance that we give to our dogs can be deemed "mood altering," including the most natural of substances such as amino acids. It's important to remember that many of the alternative therapies are not regulated and might not have actually been proven to be effective. Moreover, some alternative substances can be downright dangerous if contraindicated for that dog – a problem that can occur when non-veterinarians experiment with multiple remedies. So, opting for alternative substances over prescription medication simply because they are more "natural" is ill-advised.

Spending months or more making little to no progress with separation anxiety is incredibly difficult on guardians and dogs alike. And waiting to use meds as a last resort can take considerable time away from achieving alone-time success. Given that studies have proven that medications can both speed up the training and benefit the dog's overall well-being, it's hard to argue against starting meds as early as possible when treating separation anxiety.

Alternative remedies

In more recent years, we have also observed a growing trend toward veterinarians using alternative nutraceuticals. A **nutraceutical** is a pharmaceutical alternative that claims functional benefits. In the U.S., nutraceuticals are generally unregulated as they fall into the same FDA category as dietary supplements.

As noted above, just because something is over-the-counter, holistic, or natural doesn't make it safe. Moreover, very few controlled studies exist to confirm the efficacy of common herbal remedies in pets. Hetts notes: "In the authors' experience, over-the-counter naturopathic remedies are not effective for the high anxiety of separation reactions. Those available by prescription only have a much better success rate." (2012) Unfortunately, owners are often swayed by their desire to believe anecdotes they may hear from friends or online that have not been subject to scientific research. The same might be said for

117

many drugs used in behavior therapy, but at least most have been proven extensively in studies of humans. Another problem with herbal remedies is that there can be considerable variation in purity and quality from one manufacturer to the next, and even from one batch to the next.

As a trainer, you need to educate yourself about the products your clients are considering using. Many natural products are sold on the internet where regulations are lax or nonexistent. As an example, I have found several websites advertising stress relief remedies for dogs that contain a tiny amount of minimally active ingredients combined with fillers, alcohol, and verifiable junk. At best, these remedies could be a waste of the owner's money; at worst, a dog could have a bad reaction to the fillers and the alcohol. So, proceed with care and make certain that scientific evidence and testing have shown the product to be useful and safe for dogs.

A few of the more common alternative remedies that are being dispensed by veterinarians (although they are available without a prescription to the consumer) are Zylkene, Solliquin, and Composure.

Zylkene contains bovine-sourced hydrolyzed milk protein, an ingredient that has calming properties.

Solliquin is a behavioral health supplement that is said to support balanced behavior and relaxation. The active ingredients in Solliquin are extracts of magnolia and phellodendron, L-theanine, and a proprietary dried whey protein concentrate.

Composure is a mixture of ingredients such as L-theanine and a colostrum complex. The ingredients are said to work synergistically to support relaxation without changing the dog's personality or energy levels.

In addition to the medications and alternative remedies there are a few products that claim to help with separation anxiety, including the ThunderShirt and the Calmer Canine.

The **ThunderShirt** is simply a tight-fitting article of clothing for the dog that is intended to apply gentle constant pressure to calm anxiety. While I have not seen much if any effectiveness for separation anxiety with this product, I also have concerns about leaving a dog alone while wearing an item of clothing like this, particularly for long durations. I feel equally concerned that if we see a calmer appearing dog that he may simply be a bit shut down. I know how many dogs cringe at their harness even though it means going for a walk, and this shirt seems like it could fall into that category, particularly if the dog is not properly conditioned to wearing it.

A more recently released product on the market is called the **Calmer Canine**. It claims to be a drug-free solution for separation anxiety. I have yet to see any significant results from the use of this product in the separation anxiety dogs I have worked with. This product uses certain targeted pulsed electromagnetic fields. While there have been few if any side effects reported, there is a question about the potency of such a device, even in human use (McKenzie, 2020).

CBD for separation anxiety in dogs

Cannabidiol, known as CBD, is a chemical compound extracted from hemp. There is no shortage of anecdotal claims about how CBD is the be-all and end-all for helping dogs with separation anxiety (and many other ailments, for that matter).

While I respect and understand people's desire to find a natural product that can help their dog with anxiety, I do feel it is extremely important that dog owners are aware of the risks of using unproven remedies that include chemicals like CBD.

Here are some important facts to consider if you are contemplating using CBD in order to support your dog with their separation anxiety:

1. **The use of CBD for anxiety in dogs is not approved by the FDA.** This may come as a surprise since there is such a tremendous wealth of CBD products and associated claims about the benefits of CBD. Interestingly, there is not a single medication containing CBD that is approved by the FDA for dogs – that is not just in reference to separation anxiety products, but for any ailment. At the time of this book's publication, there is only one medicinal product even approved for humans that includes CBD.

2. **Regulation of quality in CBD is not required.** These products are classified as "supplements," not "drugs." As supplements, no tests are required to verify the purity or safety of CBD products or even to confirm the reliability of testing that a manufacturer may have done. It should be further noted that in addition to these products not being subjected to any

regulatory oversight, the manufacturers of CBD products are not able to legally make any claims regarding diagnosis, cure, mitigation, treatment, or prevention of any disease. As you may have noticed, though, they do. Since 2015 and yearly since then, the FDA has sent out letters to many of these manufacturers for their false, illegal claims.

In 2017, a study published in the *Journal of the American Medical Association* discovered that CBD/hemp products were frequently mislabeled. The products were shown to often contain much more or less CBD than reported. The JAMA study found that the amount of CBD in the products studied was incorrectly labeled 69% of the time, even when allowing for a 10% variance. (The findings showed that 42.9% had less CBD than labeled and 26.2% had more than labeled.) Additionally, undisclosed THC (which is dangerous to dogs) was found in 21.4% of the samples tested. From a purity standpoint many of these products also contained other substances that are possibly toxic to dogs. Some even contained xylitol, which is deadly to dogs. Owners should be aware that any CBD supplement given to a dog to consume should have a certificate of analysis (COA) that confirms the amounts of cannabinoids (hemp-derived substances) present. The COA should come from a third party, not the manufacturer itself.

3. **Research on CBD is extremely limited and has only just recently scratched the surface.** Fans of CBD products believe that they may have benefits in relieving pain, nausea, anxiety, depression, seizure activity and more, yet not one of these benefits for animals has been proven. Because of legal limitations on availability of actual cannabinoids, pharmaceutical companies wanting to conduct research and investigation were limited to using synthetic versions as opposed to the actual product until recently. "Hemp" classified products were removed from the controlled substance list under the 2018 Farm Bill. Prior to the passing of that bill, the ability to research CBD in labs was significantly compromised.

4. **Correct dosage and concentration amounts are entirely unknown for use in dogs.** As mentioned, there is no legally required pre-sale testing or oversight of the production or labeling of supplements. Additionally, because of the lack

of sufficient research, there has been no discovery of dosage information for use in dogs for any ailment, including anxiety. While cannabidiol is thought to be less toxic than some other compounds in marijuana, there is still risk in that insufficient research has been conducted. The lack of research means that no dosage information has been discovered and unfortunately, all one needs to do is look at social media threads to see that owners are giving largely different dosages to their dogs, ranging from miniscule to massive.

5. **The use of a supplement like CBD is potentially contraindicated with various other supplements and medications.** Without sufficient research and investigation of CBD products, the potential exists for problematic interactions to happen with other supplements or medication. One of the more recent FDA warnings sent out in late 2019 specifically states that CBD can affect the body's metabolism of other drugs, causing serious side effects.

6. **Dogs have high numbers of cannabinoid receptors, much higher than humans.** Because of the difference in receptors, the effect that CBD may have on dogs is likely different than it is in humans. Dogs may be more susceptible to toxicity. (Tschorn, 2017)

7. **By law, veterinarians cannot prescribe or dispense CBD.** At the time of publication, only veterinarians in California, Colorado, and Oregon are able to *discuss* the use of CBD in pets – in all other states they are legally prohibited from doing so. Any product that will be administered to a dog for medicinal purposes should be discussed with a veterinarian; however, at this time it is not legal for most veterinarians to discuss CBD use, let alone prescribe or dispense it. The situation is truly buyer beware for CBD products.

8. **The potential for liver injury with CBD usage has been identified.** The FDA identified certain safety risks, including the potential for liver injury. This serious risk can be managed when humans take an FDA-approved CBD drug product under medical supervision, but it is less clear how it might be managed when CBD is used without medical supervision and not in accordance with FDA-approved labeling, which is how it is currently being used by dog

owners. This was the information given by the FDA in their warning issued in November 2019.

9. **Warnings have been issued to pet CBD manufacturers about the way in which the product can be used.** There is specific language that cannot be used by manufacturers of CBD products. Despite the laws being stringent on prohibiting marketing language to not include terminology such as "treat," "cure," "acute," "disease," and "chronic," manufacturers have continually been issued warnings yearly since 2015 due to violation of these regulations. A 2018 article published in *Cannabis Business Executive* was entitled "How to Market CBD Products in the Sea of Uncertainty." The article offered tips to companies wanting to sell CBD-containing products, including what words could be used to imply medical benefits without using the forbidden terminology. The marketing of these products is profound and widespread.

10. **Cannabis toxicity reports are on the rise in the U.S., including those from CBD-only products.** In the U.S., toxicity reports have been rising about dogs having dangerous reactions to various cannabis products. The ASPCA Animal Poison Control Center has seen dogs develop the same clinical signs after ingesting CBD-only products as from ingesting THC.

The above reasons to me are sufficient deterrent for steering clear of cannabidiol products for dogs at this time. For those of you who want a healthy dose of evidence-based research in order to support what you are administering to your dog, it looks like there is a little bit of a wait ahead for you. I like the statement that Dr. Ken Pawslowski, immediate past president of the California Veterinary Medical Association, gave for an article in the *Los Angeles Times*. "It's like the Wild West out there," he said. "They might as well be buying something from the kid on the corner, because that's as much information as anybody has."

Working with veterinarians

Because of the complexity of separation anxiety, it is highly recommended that dog trainers, owners, and vets all collaborate on the issue (Turner, 1997). Numerous cases will require the use of behavior pharmacology, and the veterinarian will have to carefully evaluate which meds or med combinations will be best for the individual dog.

Working with vets is important for many types of behavior issues, and if you are a vet reading this book, thank you for doing what you do; you are so appreciated!

It is not the job of the trainer to diagnose separation anxiety, but rather to provide the vet sufficient information about the behavior(s) that were observed during the assessment. Notice that I mention here *observed* behavior. We talked about this a little in the section about relaying information to the client, but it bears repeating. Telling the vet that the dog looked worried is not useful, but explaining that you saw the dog pace, pant, and whine is.

The following section was written by Dr. Amy Pike who is a veterinarian in Virginia. She has been such a pleasure to work with and I am so grateful to be able to include this section in the book.

Amy Pike on the veterinary behaviorist's role in separation anxiety

My name is Amy Pike, and I am a veterinarian and a board-certified veterinary behaviorist. What does that mean, exactly? I can diagnose, treat, and prescribe for animals of *all* species (seriously, like at least 10 different types of animal that I can think of off the top of my head). But my passion is small animal behavior medicine, specifically treating patients (mostly dogs and cats) with behavior issues including aggression, compulsive disorders, panic disorders, and fear, and prescribing medication and behavior modification to help my patients achieve more normal lives. A veterinary behaviorist is the equivalent of a human psychiatrist, meaning I can both diagnose and prescribe medication. By the way, I like using human analogies with my clients so they can better understand things from their pets' perspective. Except for the fact that our patients cannot talk to us, and they come to see us attached to their owners, it is essentially the same. We diagnose and treat emotional disorders. And just like our human counterparts, we do not work in a vacuum. We rely on the help of other professionals to treat the patient, first and foremost on the patient's family veterinarian to ensure the pet's general health is addressed.

Pets should *always* be seen first by their family veterinarian whenever a behavior concern is identified. The family veterinarian (also known as a general practitioner or primary care veterinarian) can diagnose and treat any underlying medical disorders that may be the root cause of the behavior, or at least a contributing factor to the behavior problem. Do not discount the role a medical issue can play in separation anxiety, even though seemingly unrelated on the surface. I have seen patients over the years whose only symptoms of underlying medical diseases were new or worsening anxiety when separated from their owner. Two cases stand out over my years of practice.

The first one is the 11-year-old German shorthaired pointer who came to see me during my residency for sudden onset of separation anxiety. The dog was ultimately diagnosed with a splenic mass. After the spleen was removed, his separation anxiety resolved (with no behavioral intervention at all). Unfortunately, pathology on the mass did come back as cancerous. Six months later, the owner contacted me for another surge in separation anxiety, and the dog was sadly diagnosed with a heart tumor, likely a result of spread from the splenic tumor. The owner opted to humanely euthanize him.

The second case is a current patient of mine, a 4-year-old pit bull named Thor who came in for such profound separation anxiety that the owners were facing eviction from their condo because of his destruction, his vocalization, and his escape into the interior hallways. He had even managed to take the elevator downstairs one day and ended up in the lobby, much to the chagrin of the owners (and the management)! Fast-forward through several months of trying to find the right medication combination for him, alongside behavior modification, and all was well in Thor's world, until his family contacted me saying that all of a sudden he was showing profound separation anxiety again. They even sent me video of him standing on their dining room table howling as loudly as he possibly could! As I questioned them about what, if anything, had changed, the only thing that sprung to their minds was that he had vomited a couple times the week before the upsurge. I recommended that they take Thor to their family veterinarian for a full work-up. Turns out, Thor had swallowed pieces of a rope toy! Their veterinarian was able to remove the pieces of rope via endoscopy (using a camera and instruments placed down the esophagus into the stomach). The owners returned to work, and Thor returned to his normal routine of sleeping on the mat next to the front door, patiently "waiting" for his owners' return. Two other times I have been called for surges of Thor's anxiety, and each time it turns out to be something related to a medical disorder of his gastrointestinal tract. Now, the owners, his family veterinarian, and I are all very well-versed in the course of action should his anxiety peak: Go straight to their family vet and look for something medical.

Once the family veterinarian has ruled out the common medical disorders that could play a role in separation anxiety, a client can then pursue a behavioral modification plan with a certified separation anxiety trainer (CSAT), the social workers of the animal field. If the trainer suspects a medical problem is contributing to the separation anxiety problem, then calling on a veterinary behaviorist to prescribe psychotropic medication for the pet when it is warranted. Many of the patients I see with separation anxiety have such profound panic attacks when the owner leaves that, without medication, training alone will be largely unsuccessful. Medications given daily like Reconcile (the dog brand of Prozac) and Clomicalm (a tricyclic antidepressant) have been shown to significantly shorten the treatment duration when combined with behavior modification. Just as is true in human medicine, when we work as a team of professionals to help a patient with behavior disorders such as separation anxiety, the owner and pet will have the best possible care and support to achieve their goals.

As I sit here finishing the writing of this, it is spring of 2020 and we are in the midst of a pandemic. Many of my clients are reporting to me that their pets are thrilled that they are home all the time. The dogs get more walks every day, they get to ride in the car to pick up the groceries, and they don't get left home alone, ever. One of the concerns I hear from veterinarians, owners, and the countless media inquiries I have responded to is "What will happen to all these pets once we all go back to work? Will all the pets suffer from separation anxiety? Will our cats start peeing all over our things, and our dogs be wreaking havoc on our homes and trying to escape out windows and doors? Will veterinary behaviorists and certified separation anxiety trainers be so overwhelmed with business that we will curse the day we ever heard the words COVID-19?" At the time of this writing, it obviously remains to be seen what exactly will transpire. However, while this is a valid concern, I suspect that many pets will tap into their innate resilience and cope, either displaying only mild anxiety signs or none at all, much like our human responses to the pandemic. Thankfully, the scientists among us are looking at this very topic. Data is being gathered all over the world about our pets' behavior during this pandemic and after. I suspect we will know even more about the risk factors for separation anxiety as well. Does spending 24/7 with your dog result in a dog who is unable to cope with departures? If the dog had mild or moderate separation anxiety prior to the pandemic, do they end up with severe separation anxiety once the owners go back to work? But, regardless of the outcomes, veterinarians, veterinary behaviorists, and the CSAT professionals will be here to help the pets and their owners as a dedicated team for the single cause of helping pets live their best lives.

Chapter 7
Separation Anxiety in
Special Situations

While there are many similarities in treatment protocols for separation anxiety across all dogs, there are a few types of dogs who fall into special categories that might require you to alter your plan in certain ways. Among these groups are dogs at either end of the age spectrum, those in multidog households, those with noise sensitivities or phobias, and those in shelter or rescue environments.

Puppies, wonderful puppies

There is absolutely nothing in the world that I find more endearing than a waft of puppy breath. It signifies all that is wholesome and pure in my mind. I know many dog lovers feel the same way that I do as well. Puppies are just that awesome.

It may come as a surprise that puppies can have separation anxiety too. When I first started working with separation anxiety, I assumed that puppies were somehow immune to separation anxiety, and I'm not sure why I felt that. Over the years, I started to see more puppies clinically diagnosed with separation anxiety, and that made me think a lot.

There is not only the evolutionary function for anxiety when separated, but since we are also now learning about the possibility of a genetic component of separation anxiety, it makes sense that it would exist even in these young beings. It appears that in the literature there is no data on the age of onset of separation anxiety in dogs, so it makes sense that it could be part of the suite of issues for some puppies (Cannas, 2010).

It bears mentioning here that puppies with separation anxiety break my heart even more than adolescent or adult dogs – that's saying a lot since I genuinely fret over every client dog! The reason puppy separation anxiety feels especially heart-rending to me is actually less about the dog and more about the puppy owner. Most every new puppy parent exists in that pink cloud of love and hope for their new bundle of joy. They certainly did not expect to be dealing with a behavior issue from the get-go. No one anticipates it; it's not supposed to be that way.

I think it's important to realize that it is neither puppy cuteness nor naivete of the owner that produces this euphoric blind sightedness of a potential problem behavior. There's a real biological influence that many people experience when faced with a puppy. For puppy lovers, the endorphins released are no less potent than the experience of falling in love or looking at a baby.

In the article "This Is Your Brain on Puppy Pictures," published by *National Geographic* in March 2017, Heather Brady states, "The leading theory, known as the 'baby schema' effect, says a release of the chemicals dopamine and oxytocin is triggered in the brain when humans look at puppies. The same chemicals are released when we look at babies, and similar chemicals are released when we fall in love."

Many new puppy owners are not emotionally prepared to be faced with a challenging behavioral condition at this juncture, and that's normal. Nonetheless, the issue exists.

Yes, puppies cry. It is normal and age-appropriate behavior. Whining puppies are not necessarily distressed puppies. When normal fussing and whining does turn into anxious displays, however, the issue must be addressed appropriately.

Unfortunately, the advice to let a puppy cry it out is harmful when it comes to distressed puppies. I realize that many professionals in the fields of both dogs and children are proponents of the cry it out method. I would like to offer my reasoning for being opposed to the method, as well as alternative suggestions for how to handle puppies who are crying during isolation.

Why not let them cry it out? Prolonged anxiety can lead to numerous issues, but the one concern I will discuss here is the potential of exacerbating fear. If a puppy is demonstrating distress when alone, and his continued cries receive no response, the result could be an increase in alone-time fear. By *response*, I am referring to a reprieve from the alone time.

What can be done instead of letting a puppy cry it out during alone time? One of my colleagues says we need to give puppies a "soft place to land." I love that illustration. This is not referring to a physically soft place (although that is good too), but rather gradually exposing them to alone time. You must be thinking, gosh, that sounds a lot like a separation anxiety protocol. Bingo!

Puppies, like adolescent or adult dogs, benefit from systematic desensitization when there is a presenting fear. A separation anxiety protocol for puppies differs only in a few aspects.

1. It is typically appropriate to start with short sessions when working with puppies. We most often break the puppy missions up into two sections of 10 to 15 minutes each.

2. Puppies need authorized stuff available for chewing. If they don't have items to keep their mouths busy, they may nibble on inappropriate things, not from anxiety, but because, well, they're puppies.

3. It is essential to have the puppy empty (pottied), before starting a mission. We are usually still working on housetraining with puppies in the early stages, so making sure we safeguard that is important.

While everything here is applicable for puppies that genuinely have separation anxiety, this protocol is suitable for any puppy in the beginning.

A common question asked of me is what can be done to prevent separation anxiety (in puppies or adult dogs). The popular term used is prevention. I prefer to use the expression "optimizing the potential for alone-time success." You may think my choice of descriptor is excessively picky, but I feel that by describing separation anxiety as preventable, we are implying that we know the precise cause. We do not. The etiology is still unclear. We cannot prevent something for which we do not know the cause. Additionally, if we claim that we can prevent separation anxiety, there is the potential to resort to owner-blaming later if the puppy does indeed end up with SA.

Optimizing the potential for alone time success with a puppy is simply about conducting a modified separation anxiety protocol. Using systematically implemented gradual exposure so as not to cause distress is the recommended process.

Geriatric dogs

The main thing that I want to mention about older dogs is that canine cognitive dysfunction can look a lot like separation anxiety, even in the early phases of its onset. Any time a dog of any age presents with a sudden onset of separation anxiety (or any behavior for that matter), there should be a vet check to ensure there is not a medical reason for the issue. Pain is a common reason that dogs display symptoms that mimic separation anxiety, but numerous physical reasons could be a medical differential diagnosis. Please have your clients consult with their veterinarian, even when it seems clear that the issue is purely behavioral. The veterinarian should be part of triage for separation anxiety and can provide ongoing support or medication when needed.

Like puppies, sometimes, it can be prudent to have shorter missions to accommodate the needs of a geriatric dog. Base the decision of whether to shorten missions on the individual dog's needs, of course.

Multidog households
There is no shortage of information available to remind us that having a second dog can be double or more the work. It would seem then, that having two or more dogs in the household might multiply the work that needs to be devoted to separation anxiety training, but fortunately, that is not precisely the case.

The simple rule to follow in a multidog household is easy to remember: Only move as fast as the least comfortable dog.

Whether you have one dog with SA amongst several housemates, or more than one dog with SA in the household, you must adjust your protocol so that you adhere to the most challenged dog. Whoever's threshold is the most conservative is the one that you will follow with your missions.

Noise phobias and noise reactivity
It is only fitting that there should be a section on noise phobias in this book, since they are considered to be highly comorbid with separation anxiety. According to Flannigan and Dodman (2001), "Results of our study indicated that a fear of noises may be more common in dogs than previously observed and that almost half of dogs with separation anxiety have this fear."

Rather than discuss this topic myself, I asked the ever kind and always brilliant Eileen Anderson to contribute the following section – I'm so grateful that she said yes!

Eileen is an award-winning author and positive reinforcement dog trainer. She writes about behavior science, her life with dogs, and training with positive reinforcement on her widely popular blog, and has published a book on canine cognitive dysfunction. She holds bachelor's and master's degrees in music performance and a master's degree in engineering science.

Eileen Anderson on noise phobia:

Separation anxiety and noise phobia or reactivity sometimes appear together, but they have different modalities of treatment. Treatment of noise phobia and reactivity is beyond the scope of this book, but it's important to know how to adjust the environment for SA treatment for a dog who is also noise phobic or reactive.

Dogs with noise phobia often react to very specific sounds. Thunder and fireworks phobias are generally well-known, but there are also a fair number of dogs who have a panic reaction to high-pitched noises such as whistles and digital beeps. It's important to know what exactly the dog's triggering noises are to protect him from them to the extent we can.

There are also reactive dogs who are triggered by noises outside the home, such as other dogs barking, delivery trucks, and human voices "too close" to the house. These dogs have a learned fear response to noises that predict things they are scared of.

Ideally, we would protect noise-phobic and noise-reactive dogs from all noises during treatment (and all the time), but this is not possible. The physics of sound prevents it. As with SA, there are many myths about how to treat noise phobia, too many to list here. Just know that, as with SA, most of the common suggestions don't work.

The best way to protect dogs from unwanted sounds is through sound masking. This is defined as creating other sounds that interfere with and inhibit us (and dogs) from hearing the problem sounds. Sound masking does not somehow *block* extraneous sound. It works because hearing requires complex brain activity, and well-designed sound masking prevents many creatures with ears from distinguishing the problem sounds from the background creating by the masking noise.

White noise machines, or playing white noise loops from YouTube over high-quality speakers, can mask a fair amount of external noise. White noise is random noise over a range of frequencies. The net effect is a kind of hissing sound. Brown noise is similar, but has more low frequencies. It sounds more like the roaring of a large waterfall. It can mask even more effectively, but those rumbling low frequencies can scare some thunder-phobic dogs. It is definitely worth trying if the dog is not triggered by low frequencies.

Music that is regularly played at home and that doesn't trigger the dog can also be used for its masking qualities. Hard rock and heavy metal (again, only if the dog isn't scared of them!) can mask some low frequencies, as can taiko drumming. One would assume that a dog scared of thunder would automatically fear these things, but many habituate to different types of music despite fears of similar noises.

Bluegrass and baroque music can be good for preventing a reactive dog from noticing higher frequencies, such as a referee's whistle or the jingling of the neighbor dog's tags. And audio books can mask the sounds of human voices. Again, one would think that a dog who reacts to the sound of human voices outside the house would also be scared of a human voice coming through speakers, but that's rarely the case. Most dogs can discriminate perfectly well between sounds in the natural environment and similar sounds coming out of speakers.

TV and radio are not good choices to leave on for masking because the programming or commercials might include sounds that trigger your dog.

Remember: Choose sounds and music for their masking qualities, not for any claimed properties of inducing relaxation. Music is not a primary reinforcer for humans, much less dogs. The studies of using music to attempt to calm dogs are scattershot and do not constitute good evidence when examined as a group. Apply the principles of acoustics to your advantage instead, by using masking.

Speaking of acoustics, I will include mention of a common recommendation that emphatically does not work. You can't protect your dog from sounds by using so-called absorbent materials. Acoustic foam, for example, is designed to "tune" the sounds in a room, not prevent sounds from entering. True soundproofing materials are very bulky, heavy, and costly. You would need a structure with soundproofed walls several feet thick (thicker than the walls of your house) to prevent most noises from entering, and several *yards* thick to protect from thunder. You just can't do it. Covering a crate with absorbent blankets or lining a closet with acoustic foam can create a space that is acoustically "dead" inside, that is, it has few reverberations. Some people and some dogs may find this effect comforting. But this setup will not block external sounds from entering.

Basements do have some soundproofing qualities, but they can be unpredictable. Most will block out the sounds of faraway storms, for instance. They are likely good for higher frequency sounds. But since sound travels exceedingly well through solids like the ground, a close lightning strike could theoretically be *louder* in the basement than above ground. Since it's best for SA dogs to stay in the area of the home in which they are most comfortable when practicing absences, putting a dog in a basement would not be recommended for this. But allowing access to it would be fine if it's part of their regular living space.

Managing the two conditions is tricky, but the recordings the client makes during absences can possibly alert you to noise triggers that could be playing a part in the dog's fear. You can incorporate careful masking into your absences if needed. And to state the obvious, you would never want to plan absences during a thunderstorm or fireworks display if your SA dog is phobic of those sounds. You can use storm tracker apps to make sure you don't schedule an absence during a time when a storm is likely, and to prompt you to head home if a storm suddenly develops.

Shelter and rescue dogs

I have had the genuine honor and pleasure to work with my colleague Casey McGee on developing some guides to best practices for shelters and rescues who have separation anxiety dogs in their care. This is just a small taste of what we have been working on with many shelters here in the U.S., but we will be releasing a full program about this soon.

Casey has graciously agreed to write this section of the book, and I'm so glad that she did, as it is truly an important piece of working with separation anxiety dogs. Casey is a 2016 honors graduate of the Academy for Dog Trainers as well as my Separation Anxiety Certification Program. Casey found her calling in force-free dog training after a career working with domestic violence and sexual assault advocates, law enforcement, and prosecution to reform the way that public institutions respond to violence against women and children. Today, she and I are collaborating with shelters and rescues to develop a best practices guide for helping homeless dogs with separation anxiety.

Casey McGee on shelter and rescue best practices:

Separation anxiety presents a unique problem to shelter and rescue workers who are tasked with saving lives with very few resources and often have to decide whether or not a dog is adoptable.

For those of you in the business of finding homeless dogs permanent homes and caring for them while they wait, you naturally worry about putting a dog with a pre-existing anxiety disorder through the transition of several foster homes or holding facilities. You've seen dogs whose qualities of life deteriorate when surrounded by chaos, who wear out their welcome in foster home after foster home, or injure themselves trying to escape from crates and kennels. You've seen dogs with labeled separation anxiety linger on the adoption floor of the shelter, waiting for a family with the perfect constellation of circumstances who's willing and able to cope with a dog who can never be left alone. It's a heart-wrenching decision, no matter how sympathetic you are to the disorder, and it can seem that the deck is stacked against these dogs.

While the challenges are real, many progressive shelters and rescues are collaborating with separation anxiety trainers and trying innovative strategies to improve the outcomes of homeless dogs with separation anxiety, with some very exciting and promising results. The details of those efforts are beyond the scope of this book, and are enumerated on the website malenademartini.com. But here we'll discuss three of the most important considerations to positive outcomes: improving your diagnostics, maintaining the dog's quality of life while in your care, and determining how to get started.

Assessing separation anxiety in the homeless dog

In many ways, separation anxiety is the canine behavior disorder whose time has come. Where 20 years ago few dog owners would have even heard of isolation distress, today it enjoys widespread recognition even though it may not yet be well understood. As a result, many people whose dogs vocalize, are destructive, or eliminate while alone often surrender dogs for reasons of "separation anxiety." Even dogs who counter-surf or have trash parties when unsupervised, or those who shadow their owners into bathrooms, are thought to have this disorder.

As mentioned earlier, differential diagnoses for separation anxiety-type symptoms include:

- Confinement anxiety
- Poor house training/chew training
- Noise phobias

- Thunder phobia
- Reaction to outside stimuli
- Transitional stress (see below)

Some dogs exhibit symptoms of separation anxiety the first few weeks in a new home, then improve spontaneously in a few weeks, given very little intervention except suspended absences and the passage of time. Generally, we recommend that dogs new to an environment be allowed a week or two to acclimate before doing assessments or attempting diagnostics.

To further confound the issue, many dogs who end up having separation anxiety in their permanent homes mysteriously show no symptoms while alone in a kennel environment, and vice versa. Ruling out all of the above requires observing the dog's behavior in a home environment that they have been in for several weeks – a tall order, indeed, but a necessity. The stakes can be very high, after all, both for false positives and false negatives.

The experiences of the dogs' previous owners are your most valuable diagnostic tool, when available. If you're not already emphasizing high-quality intake interviews at the point of owner surrender, do so. Train the staff tasked with this job and support them with forms designed to tease out the most obvious rule-outs. Create the kind of surrender environment in which owners are most likely to want to participate. Consider requiring appointments for surrenders.

Absent historical information, if you suspect a dog might have separation anxiety but are unsure, try to get him into a foster home for a few weeks before videotaping a few short absences.

Maintaining quality of life

As we've mentioned, plenty of dogs who later turn out to have separation anxiety do survive the kennel just fine. It's how they slip through our fingers undiagnosed, after all, not showing symptoms in the shelter. Others do show quite a bit of anxiety, and can deteriorate physically and behaviorally over time. Shelter and rescue staff will have had experience with dogs who put up increasing resistance to return to their kennels (even sometimes to the point of aggression), have chronic unresolved GI issues and can't keep on the weight, or are injuring themselves trying to escape. A deteriorating quality of life is a dealbreaker for many, and we agree with that assessment. Here are a few strategies to consider.

Minimize dogs' alone time. This requires creativity and a patchwork quilt approach, but this is where infrastructure and planning ahead will save the day. Consider building a foster care network for special needs dogs, whose members can stay closely connected to dog sit and support each other when needed. Enlist volunteers who can't be proper foster homes but still want to help to lessen the burden on the full-time foster homes, and cover evenings or weekend days. Encourage desk fostering and sleepovers with volunteers and staff. Approach area daycares for pro bono or discounted spots when appropriate, in exchange for promoting the business to adopters.

Don't shy away from using anti-anxiety medications. Many shelters and rescues are creatively leveraging both short-term and long-term anxiolytics to manage a dog's quality of life while he's in their care. We're lucky to have available decades of research on how these kinds of medications have direct application to canine separation anxiety, so their use should not be considered fringe, experimental or as a last resort. If your shelter or rescue's consulting veterinarian would like to learn more about the options available, please see Chapter 6 or consult Karen Overall's 2013 *Manual of Clinical Behavioral Medicine for Dogs and Cats*.

Heavily emphasize enrichment, human interaction, and exercise. Forge relationships with dog walkers in your area (also in exchange for promoting them) who can take these dogs on marathon outings. Enrichment won't cure these dogs' anxiety, obviously, but it will promote rest when they're alone and it will take the babysitting load off the foster home or administrative staff.

Please note that, except as forms of enrichment, relaxation protocols, obedience training, and non-shadowing training have very little impact on this panic disorder, particularly within the shelter environment. Many agencies with behavior staff are attempting early desensitization protocols with dogs with separation anxiety, which is a lovely thought, but it may have mixed long-term value.

We think that desensitization may have good value to potential adopters when you can say with all credibility, "Blue has shown that she responds to desensitization. She has already progressed from X to Y." Moreover, early progress will be prognostically favorable, and maybe more importantly sets a precedent for training strategies that will hopefully circumvent them trying misguided strategies read online or given as advice from friends. And lastly, a desensitization protocol may progress more quickly the second time through.

However, desensitization conducted in a shelter or foster home environment may have minimal value to the dog. After all, you've learned that desensitization in the early stages is very context-specific: "I've learned to relax when X person walks out Y door wearing her jacket but not carrying her purse." Bottom line, compared to other demands on your volunteer and staff time, and the relative value of suspending absences and enrichment, you may want to deprioritize training until the dog finds his permanent home.

Pick your battles

Rescues don't need to take every special needs dog that crosses their path, but you'll find that shoring up your organizational commitment at the management level and having a prepared infrastructure will vastly improve your success. Start small and experience some positive outcomes so that your funders, stakeholders, staff, and volunteers see the benefit of the new strategies. Select a few dogs who are most likely to be easily adopted. In these early stages, consider beginning with dogs who:

- Respond well to being kenneled
- Are prosocial to all people, dogs, and cats (so that you have the widest number of daycare or dogsitting options)
- Are candidates for anti-anxiety medication
- Have no other chronic medical issues

Remember that the severity of isolation-related behaviors does not necessarily equate to the speed with which the dog will respond to training or medication. It's tempting to consider dogs who jump out of second-story windows or who cut up their faces during kennel escapes as lost causes, and way beyond the capacity of your average adoptive home, but the severity of the symptoms does not always translate to a more complicated case. We encourage you to not consider this factor when selecting the dogs with whom you begin this work.

Chapter 8
Case Studies and Stories Written by CSATs

While I find talk of protocols and data, along with the emotional highs and lows of treating separation anxiety, to be fascinating and compelling (and I hope you do too), I think individual stories can help paint a fuller picture of what this work actually looks like. In this chapter, some CSATs have been generous enough to share their stories so that readers of this book can understand the process more fully. I'm grateful for their contribution.

Oliver's story – Tiffany Lovell (technology)

Oliver and his parents were my first overseas clients. Living in Amsterdam, they were both originally from America and had adopted Oliver from a breeder once they relocated. Oliver, or Ollie as they called him, was a gorgeous young Golden Retriever with a lovely temperament and easygoing personality. Except, of course, if he was left home alone. His parents quickly determined that Ollie was struggling when they would leave, even if he had plenty of toys and yummy treats as all the books said to leave for him. He was whining, barking, and howling, and it was quite loud for the neighbors. He would also pace throughout their apartment searching for them and was simply unable to settle and relax the entire time they were gone. In addition to the concern over neighbor complaints, Ollie's parents were distraught about the idea that he was obviously miserable if left alone.

As luck would have it, Ollie's mom knew an awesome dog trainer back in the States. It was her aunt in California, who owned her own successful training business specializing in puppies. When she reached out for guidance regarding Ollie's anxiety, her aunt immediately knew they needed to work with a CSAT.

That's where I came in. The prospect of my first overseas clients had me both excited and a bit nervous. Would the time difference prove to be too challenging for all our busy schedules? Would the technology cooperate or fail us? I also felt a little added pressure because of their family member being a professional trainer, so I had to get this right.

We began as all CSAT cases do, with an initial live video conferencing session via Zoom. It worked great! Ollie's parents were wonderful and completely on board for whatever they needed to do to help their sweet boy feel more relaxed and comfortable. I learned that Mom frequently traveled for work and Dad worked from home.

They had already arranged for Ollie to be with a neighbor when he couldn't be with one of them. This neighbor also happened to be the guardian of Ollie's best friend, a dog named Buddy. So, as you can imagine, he was more than happy to spend time there.

Ollie's parents and I quickly and easily figured out our schedules, even with the extended time difference and it became a non-issue. Even when his mom was traveling in another city, we could easily meet via Zoom from three different locations for our weekly check-ins. How cool is that?!

I was also pleasantly surprised when Ollie's dad chose to set up other camera angles within their apartment using Zoom and multiple devices they already had, like tablets and cell phones. This allowed us to see where Ollie moved during their practice missions and while we all watched during our weekly live assessments. We had a total of four different views and could watch Ollie's movement. This was quite helpful, especially early on. While it was fantastic to have all of the various camera angles and we benefited from their inclusion, I should note that many of my clients have only one view available, and we absolutely make that work just fine.

Ollie progressed nicely through the training protocol, hitting a few regressions along the way, as almost all dogs do. But his amazingly dedicated parents and I continued to work through these speed bumps together as a team, giving Ollie "easy wins" when he needed them and watching closely whenever we pushed forward in duration.

We celebrated every milestone along the way, including the moment Ollie became so relaxed and calm that he fell asleep on his bed for over an hour. (His initial starting relaxed time was only a few seconds so this was a really big deal!) Once we reached a stage where his parents felt comfortable practicing without my day-to-day guidance, they did an excellent job working to extend the duration of their absences, and Ollie continued to progress beautifully. It's hard to believe that it's been more than three years since I worked with Team Ollie, and I'm happy to report that everyone is still doing great! In fact, I see that Ollie has a new little human sister whom he apparently adores, and I couldn't be happier for them.

My first overseas separation anxiety case was one I will never forget for many reasons. First, it showed me that through technology we are able to help so many more people and dogs than we once could. It also proved that people all over the world are dedicated to their pets and want the best for them. As a bonus, I was able to learn a little about a country I'd never visited. I look forward to this happening now with each new overseas client I work with. Having the opportunity to make a difference in the lives of dogs and their humans is why I became a trainer. In my wildest dreams, I never imagined those dogs and humans would be on several different continents all over the world!

Oliver

Willa's story – Jane Wolfe (warmups)

When Kathryn and Eric adopted Willa, they were her third home in just 18 months. It was clear very quickly that Willa struggled to be alone. When they tried to leave the house, Willa would begin to panic almost immediately, running from room to room whining and howling. Willa also struggled with a lot of generalized anxiety and reactivity on leash. Kathryn and Eric quickly reached out for help from the local vet behaviorist and a local trainer. While they did get her generalized anxiety better managed, they were unable to make much if any progress in her separation anxiety. They tried just about everything: Kongs, puzzle toys, music, calming scents and sprays, relaxation protocols, and additional medications, but after six months they were exhausted and decided to suspend absences indefinitely.

I first met the family as students in my Reactive Rover class. Willa did amazingly well, and we kept in contact after class. With her reactivity under control, Eric and Kathryn were ready to try introducing her to another dog. I helped with Willa's very first ever dog playdate in her new home – turns out Willa *loves* other dogs! Because of this she was able to start going to daycare. This really changed things by giving them more flexibility in their lives. I invited Malena to do a seminar on separation anxiety in the summer of 2018, and despite their decision to cease training, they came. We reconnected at that seminar and I started working with them soon after. In the beginning Kathryn and Eric were unable to even get out the door without Willa panicking and attempting to dart past them. I started as I normally do – taking out all pre-departure cues and slowly lengthening the time out the door.

We used many easy warmup steps in the beginning of a training session to get Willa increasingly bored with her parents. Warmup steps are a valuable tool that allowed us to practice mini-departures – small versions of the ultimate goal. These steps allowed us to work up to the final "harder" step of the goal time out the door (for example, 30 seconds). Once Willa was comfortable with her parents being out the door for a couple minutes, we began to work in all the departure cues like shoes, keys, coats, and the car. I continued to use warmup steps to toggle between harder and easier steps.

Typically, when a dog is up to around 20 to 30 minutes out the door, I will start to significantly lessen the number of warmup steps, often eliminating them altogether. That way the owner's absence looks as real-life as possible. But for Willa, those warmup steps remained very important. It normally took her at least a couple warmups to relax and go park herself on the couch. Once there, she could stay relaxed in the house alone for long stretches of time. Unlike most cases, even when we got up to about 4 to 5 hours, they still had to do at least three warmups for her to settle in.

During the fall of that year, Willa had a major regression and went back to being comfortable with an absence of just a few seconds. It turned out to be a very long regression. Getting Willa back on track meant looking at the data we had collected to identify what made things harder or easier for her. We tweaked missions and tried many things that might help get back to long departures: more warmup steps, fewer warmup steps, staggering her parents' departures, time of day, and exercise beforehand. For Willa, time of day, who was leaving the house, and the number of warmup steps all seemed to make a significant difference. After identifying those parameters, we were able to make adjustments in the training mission. These adjustments made it easier for Willa and made it clearer what parameters we needed to work on.

After many months of inching along (and another visit to the vet for an adjustment to her medications) we found that if we did the exact same warmups every time, Willa would relax and remain calm for many minutes. This is not typically my approach (in fact, I haven't had a case like this since!). I typically keep the steps somewhat random to keep the dog from guessing what is coming next. For Willa, however, we found predictability was key. We broke down her parents' departure into four steps, and soon those minutes turned into hours and we got back up to about four hours out the door.

Our warmup routine was the following four steps, in this order:

- Step 1: Put on shoes and coat, grab bag and keys, step out for 10 seconds, and return.
- Step 2: Put on coat, grab bag and keys, step out, open gate across driveway (leave it open), and return.
- Step 3: Put on coat, grab bag and keys, open garage door, start then stop the car, and return.
- Step 4: Put on coat, grab bag and keys, walk out to the car, and drive away!

Willa would normally follow for the first step, then lie on a chair or couch after the second step, then remain there the rest of the time. She would get increasingly relaxed after each warmup step, usually putting her head down or sprawling out. After a few months of this we dropped one warmup step, but without at least two, Willa was unable to relax.

Today, Willa will can be alone for 3 to 4 hours at a time. A few things remain a challenge for her, including Eric and Kathryn leaving together and evening absences. They still do their two warmup steps prior to leaving. For Step 1, they put on their shoes and coat, grab their bag and keys, step out for a few seconds (this can vary now!) and then come back. For Step 2, they open the garage and the gate across the driveway and then return. By this point Willa has usually found a comfortable spot on the couch and is curled up, and then they can drive away! With all of Willa's ups and downs there is no hurry to eliminate warmups altogether, and I suspect we never will. Unlike most cases at this point, warmups remain extremely helpful.

There is always a way to make a mission easier – something you can tweak or drop or adjust to start making progress again. I often joke that the only rule to separation anxiety training is that there are no rules (except keeping the dog comfortable, of course). Willa was a challenging case. It took a lot of data tracking, creativity, and of course patience. Her owners, Kathryn and Eric, are truly incredible people and we couldn't have made the progress we did without their perseverance and trust in the process.

The warmup steps Willa's family does now are just their normal leaving routine, broken into two parts. For Willa's family, the couple extra minutes it takes to get out the door pay off bigtime if it means they can then leave for multiple hours at a time. Heck, many people often find themselves running in and out of the door a few times each morning to grab forgotten items!

Willa

While I would love to have people ultimately leave in a "normal" fashion, if including a couple quick warmup steps makes the difference between minutes or hours out the door, I think they're worth it—and many owners do too.

Chile's story – Tina Flores (clinical SA)

When I adopted Chile, she was approximately eight weeks old (this was almost 17 years ago), and I was not yet a professional trainer. I had no idea back then that there were professionals who might be able to help me, so I was left to try to muddle through on my own when Chile presented with all the "classic" symptoms of separation anxiety. She would bark, howl, and cry any time I left the room. She wouldn't eat while alone, although she is an absolute chowhound in any other situation. She caused more destruction than I ever thought a 12-pound Dachshund could do and inflicted harm on herself at the same time.

I speak with people every week who observe many of the same symptoms in their dogs, and they often tell me the same thing: "We've tried *everything!*" Although they can't see me at the other end of the phone line, I'm nodding my head because I vividly remember being in the same place. I also felt like I had tried every possible solution that I had either read about or heard from various sources. Some of the "remedies" such as diffusing essential oils, Thundershirts, or leaving out food puzzles and items of clothing that smelled like me made no difference at all to Chile's reaction upon being left alone. Some supposed solutions, however, were actually harmful. Like many dogs suffering from separation anxiety, Chile also had confinement anxiety. Sadly, one of the most common pieces of advice people receive on how to help dogs feel comfortable while alone is to put them in a crate. For Chile, this was possibly the worst thing I could have done. Her level of anxiety while confined skyrocketed to the point that she eliminated in the crate, tore off two of the wire bars, and squeezed through a space so small she bruised her ribs in the process. I tried leaving her in a room instead, which led to her injuring herself as she tried to get around the barrier. So, while she couldn't be left alone free in the house, she also could not be crated or confined in any way either. This was when I finally realized that she could not be left alone at all while we worked on finding a real solution.

At first, I had the luxury of being able to take Chile everywhere with me. I was in college, so she would just sit in my lap while I went to classes, attend parties with me, and sleep under my desk while I pulled all-nighters studying for tests. But after I graduated and got a full-time job, I knew I really needed to find help. Many dogs who panic when left alone are just fine, or at least considerably less anxious, as long as there is a person with them. The guardians of these dogs can leave them with a neighbor, friend, family member, dog walker, daycare, etc. Chile, however, was not one of these dogs. She had what is known as clinical separation anxiety. Although she was an extremely confident dog in every other aspect, she would go into a full-blown panic whenever I was not around, regardless of who else was there with her. This presented a whole different challenge. Because I couldn't be with her all the time, before I could even begin to start working on her alone time, I needed to find a way to help Chile feel just as confident when she was left with other people as she was with me. I was fortunate enough that my new job came with the opportunity to meet some amazing humans who would be incredibly helpful with the management aspect and thus instrumental in helping Chile and me overcome her fear of alone time. Many of these people are still some of my best friends, and one of them also became my husband.

My first step in helping Chile feel comfortable being left with someone besides me was showing her that these people could also be boatloads of fun! We would go over to our friends' houses, and they would shower her with attention and lots of yummy treats that she normally didn't get from me. It took some time, but I started to see some subtle changes in Chile's demeanor around certain people. One of the first significant differences I noticed was when we were at our neighbors' house. I went to the bathroom, and instead of following me as she always did, Chile actually stayed in the living room playing with them! It might sound like a very minor thing, but this was a massive breakthrough for us. We gradually worked up to my actually leaving her in the house with them. She got to the point where she would still whine a bit after I left but could quickly be distracted with treats or a fun game. One thing I found with Chile was that even though she was very comfortable around whoever was going to be staying with her, watching me leave her somewhere was still a challenge. So whenever possible, we arranged for her to be picked up from our house or even had the person meet me at the car to take her inside, and that made the separation easier for her.

Once we were finally at a place where absences could be managed with the help of friends, family, and sitters, I was able to start working on desensitizing her to being left alone by implementing gradual departures. We eventually got to the point where Chile can now be left alone comfortably for hours. However, I look back at that time and still remember how, even with all the help I had with managing her alone time, I still felt very isolated and unsure during the training process. Any behavior modification always comes with ups and downs, but I also know that had I had a professional trainer on the road with me, it would have been much less bumpy. The struggles and triumphs Chile and I faced with her separation anxiety are what led me to become a Certified Separation Anxiety Trainer. It gives me so much joy to be able to support my clients daily, so they never have to feel like they are going through this journey alone.

Chile

Milo's story – Josh Boutelle (medication and prompt attention to SA onset)

Milo is a 10-year-old Spinone Italiano. For those of you who are not familiar with the breed, they are a lanky sporting dog with fabulous wiry fur.

After losing a lifelong companion dog, Milo started to exhibit signs of anxiety whenever he was left alone. While not all dogs become anxious after the loss of a companion, for some, the effects are grave and can result in various forms of anxiety. Milo would pace, howl, and scratch at baseboards whenever his parents would leave home. Prior to his best doggy friend passing, he would go upstairs into a bedroom and take a nap for any absence, be it 30 minutes or six hours. As you can imagine, the sudden change in Milo's behavior was distressing to his parents. Milo was lucky, though. Despite the grief that his mom and dad were experiencing, they jumped into action. They got Milo help before he had a chance to form a further undesirable association with alone time.

Clever and compassionate owners that they are, Milo's parents went directly to their vet to run extensive tests to confirm there wasn't an underlying health issue. It is imperative that any dog who has a sudden change in behavior be medically screened to rule out the possibility of potential physical concerns. We cannot treat a medical condition with a behavioral solution, ever.

The vet was forward-thinking and concerned about Milo's overall welfare. Fortunately, Andrea and Greg were also open-minded to doing whatever was necessary to help their beloved boy.

After Milo was prescribed daily medication for anxiety, Andrea and Greg also immediately began managing Milo's alone time so that he was never by himself to experience distress or panic. Truly, they did everything right from the get-go, and I was fortunate enough that they contacted me to help them begin a training protocol for behavior modification. We proceeded with implementing a plan of gradual desensitization.

Milo and his parents began working with me, and we started daily missions to desensitize Milo to tiny increments of time alone in addition to the measured introduction of any departure cues that indicated that alone time was imminent.

While it is not the typical pace of every protocol, we were able to build Milo's alone time up to a consistent 4 hours(!) within one month. In this time, we successfully helped Milo go back to his old ways of napping in the window seat. Some might consider this fast progress to be merely a result of a dog that "got over" missing his buddy, but I would claim otherwise. Had Milo's parents not intervened early and continued to test the waters to see if he would recover, it is entirely possible that we would not have seen the rapid progress we were able to achieve. You might think that such early intervention is excessive or even premature, but I beg you to reconsider your thoughts. If Andrea and Greg had not immediately interceded with Milo's anxiety behaviors, there is a likelihood that his suffering could have been prolonged. The amount of time, money, and emotional bandwidth needed to put forth could have been far greater over the long haul.

It can be incredibly difficult for a dog owner to accept that a once confident dog could develop separation-related anxiety so quickly. Owners often want to try and try and try before bringing in help or using any pharmacological supplementation – sometimes for months or even years. Unfortunately, this can have a significant negative impact on the speed at which a dog recovers, which means that we are prolonging distress for both the dog and the people who love him.

Unquestionably, Milo's parents were thrilled with the outcome of all of their efforts. I hope that Milo's story inspires others to see that waiting to implement critical elements of a protocol can be a weighty error. Postponing the incorporation of medication, management, and training is simply a recipe for delaying the attainment of the alone-time success that is so desperately needed for both dog and owner alike.

Murphy's story – Lisa Waggoner (confinement)

Murphy is an adorable chocolate Aussiedoodle with the kindest eyes imaginable. He was an effervescent adolescent dog who continually exuded happiness, except when left home alone. Even as a puppy, Murphy had been a bit vocal when he was left alone in his crate.

Murphy came from a breeder and lived in a lovely suburban home with his guardians, Dawn and Brian, and their two children. He'd been given the very best start in life and enjoyed positive training and puppy socialization classes before continuing his education into basic and intermediate dog training classes.

This handsome boy easily chilled in the crate with the door open during the day at home with his guardians, and he enjoyed sleeping in his crate at night (with the door open). However, when he was left home alone with the crate door closed, he just wasn't comfortable. The family was perplexed at why he could be so happy in the crate at certain times and not at all at other times.

Dawn worked from home most days, so there was no need to crate Murphy except for the short times she was away. Dawn sensed that Murphy wasn't happy in the crate, but since he was an adolescent, she wasn't comfortable leaving him free in the house for fear he might be tempted to use his mouth on household furniture or rugs. So, what to do?

With plenty of forethought, planning, and preparation, Brian built a large plywood confinement area in the basement so Murphy could have more space to move about. If Murphy was uncomfortable in his crate, maybe he'd be happier in a larger space. And he could easily access their fenced backyard through a doggy door in the enclosure. As the basement wasn't heated, Brian added heat ducts through the top of the enclosure so Murphy would have heat. The area was complete with a bed and a few of his favorite toys. And each time Murphy was put into the basement confinement area, he'd get a treat. Yet he still wasn't comfortable, as evidenced by what they saw when watching him on camera each time they left the house. Although they were never sure of the exact moment Murphy left the enclosure, by the time they could remotely access the camera, he was outside in the January weather. The few times they did witness him going back inside the enclosure, he was whining. Each time Dawn and Brian would return home and let Murphy out, his greeting behavior was frantic. He still wasn't comfortable being left home alone.

This family was not to be deterred! Because Dawn understood Murphy just wasn't comfortable home alone in his crate and also not comfortable in the basement area, she hoped that doggy day care would be a good option. Murphy could enjoy playing with other dogs during the times the family was away.

But he wasn't comfortable at daycare either. After only a short period of time on the first day, Dawn was called to come pick up Murphy. The owner of the facility recognized his anxious behavior, suspected separation anxiety, and referred Dawn to me for separation anxiety training.

We kicked off our work together with my observing Murphy in his crate while Dawn left the house. Murphy was happy and comfortable going into his crate. He showed no concern when the crate door was closed and quickly lay down and was quiet. Ah, but not for long. Murphy began lip-licking, yawning, and fidgeting, and in less than a minute he was whining, then growling, and in a short period of time, howling. Definitely a sign of discomfort.

I also wanted to observe Murphy in the basement confinement area to see how he responded to an absence there, so we planned another assessment a day later in the basement area. Dawn gathered her belongings, set them on the kitchen counter, put a hard treat in a Kong, and led Murphy to the basement confinement area. She opened the door and put the Kong inside, and Murphy entered quite willingly, then she closed the door and left the house. Murphy stayed engaged with the Kong, but as soon as he had eaten the food, he began pacing. He'd go outside through the doggy door, pace slowly outside, go back inside and scratch at the enclosure door. He continued to repeat this sequence of behaviors, which escalated to whining during pacing and more frequent scratching at the inside of the door. When Dawn returned and let Murphy out, he was frenzied in his barking and jumping behavior and needed to be put on leash to walk upstairs.

Most dogs with separation anxiety also display confinement anxiety. In the all the years I've been working with dogs with separation anxiety, only once have I included a crate or small confinement area. The dog's progress is usually much faster when free in the house. While I shared this with Dawn, she was concerned about the possibility of Murphy getting into things around the house if he wasn't confined. Although Dawn strongly preferred to help him learn to be comfortable in the basement enclosure, she was willing to begin separation anxiety training with Murphy in his crate (in the main area of the home). I felt the common area of the home would be much more comfortable than the new, box-like plywood structure in the basement. Though I was doubtful, I designed a very detailed, systematic counter-conditioning protocol for her to work on daily for the basement enclosure (without absences).

After only two weeks into the separation anxiety training with Murphy in the crate, we had reached two to three minutes with Murphy comfortable. In reality, that's a lot of success for most dogs with separation anxiety! However, I suspected that Murphy would make even bigger strides if he were out of his crate and free in the house. Thankfully Dawn was ready to give this "freedom" plan a shot. However, she was still committed to trying to make the basement confinement area work, so she continued that daily training too. Trust me, that's a lot of commitment.

On the day of the "free in the house" assessment, I assured Dawn that because I'd be watching while she was away, there was no need to worry about any damage being done to her home by the teeth of an adolescent dog. If I had even the slightest bit of concern, I'd text her to return (and she was very close by). Imagine how pleased I was that Murphy was comfortable for a full 15 minutes! Murphy moved around the house a little bit, but for most of the time he was lying down and relaxed. What a joy!

While Dawn continued the daily counter-conditioning to the basement confinement area (which was progressing ever-so-slowly), she began giving Murphy freedom in the main living area of the house when doing the daily separation anxiety training. A short two weeks later we had reached an hour and a half absence! We were halfway to Dawn's goal of three hours.

Now to add in a dog walker. If Dawn needed to be away for a full three hours, the walker could arrive midway in that time span, and when Murphy was returned home, he'd be alone for only another hour and a half. There's a systematic way to incorporate a dog walker into a separation anxiety training plan, and we found a reputable walker to work with us to achieve our goal.

With such amazing progress free in the house, Dawn finally decided to forego the focus on Murphy's comfort in the basement area. In just another two weeks we had reached two hours. Dawn felt she had gained enough knowledge from our daily work together that she was now ready to continue training on her own. I agreed she was ready to spread her wings.

We stayed in touch and I was always pleased to hear how Murphy was gaining in comfort with longer and longer absences (both at home and at daycare). Today, Murphy is fully recovered. He's home alone up to eight hours a day with a dog walker to break up the day, and he spends his time chilling around the house. Oh, the difference freedom can make!

Murphy

Dexter's story – Casey McGee (noise phobia)

Dexter the hound mix was adopted at the age of 9 from a shelter. The first time his family left him alone, he left the house via a doggy door and scaled the 6-foot fence to escape the back yard. Naturally, the family closed the doggy door the second time they left him alone. That time, Dexter climbed up onto the kitchen counter, broke the screen out of a window and again jumped over the fence to escape the back yard.

But during a videotaped assessment of Dexter while alone, he calmly watched his family leave from the front window then climbed up on the couch and napped for an hour. Dexter's family began to closely monitor his behavior during short absences and collect data in an attempt to find patterns that would explain the discrepancy. On some days he paced, howled, and attempted escapes again, damaging windows. On other days he slept comfortably with no outward signs of distress.

Dexter's family struggled to figure out how to proceed as they were not in a position to suspend all absences for longer than a few weeks, and worried that it would be extremely difficult if not impossible to rehome him. The situation looked dire.

Dexter

One day soon after, the family tried out a new air fryer and when the beeping started, Dexter ran into the back yard and tried to scale the fence. He could not be coaxed to return to the house that evening. A few days later, a smoke detector began to chirp with a low-battery indicator and Dexter urinated on the spot and hid in the basement, refusing to return upstairs.

Due to recent research suggesting a correlation between noise anxieties and musculoskeletal pain (Lopes Fagundes et al., 2018), Dexter's vet conducted a thorough pain assessment and discovered that Dexter likely suffered from pain in his hips. After being treated for that pain, Dexter began to stay at home alone for full work days with no issues, and remains symptom-free to this day.

Holly's story: overcoming SA is possible (by Malena)

Profound lessons can be learned even many years into one's journey.

Holly is a petite little girl in a Beagle package. Her soulful eyes and demure posture melt my heart every single time I see her. Despite her unassuming appearance, she became one of my greatest teachers.

The research had always divulged for me the following lesson. Many of my cases before and after Holly further supported my belief. It was Holly herself, though, who instilled in me this core certainty.

Separation anxiety is fixable!

Holly

I received an email from Deb and Rob several years ago. They had been referred to me by the lovely Nicole Wilde, who told them that I could help them with Holly's separation anxiety.

Deb was full of fire from the moment we were in contact. Rob, while equally passionate, was a man of poise who weighed out options carefully. Together they were quite the dynamic duo.

155

We began working together on Holly's separation anxiety in September of 2013. In our initial assessment, I learned a lot about Holly's history through Deb's effervescent chatting and Rob's composed accounts of all that had transpired with her separation anxiety.

When we began our absence assessment in earnest, it was mere seconds after Deb and Rob exited the house that Holly started to bark and scratch at the door. Mind you, "bark" is an imprecise description of the mournful Beagle bellow that came from little Holly's anxious body.

It took several weeks to build up a bit of successful duration, but as most dogs do, Holly was progressing slowly but surely.

We had accomplished 11 minutes of alone time and were ecstatic. Then our first regression hit. It was a doozie. Holly suddenly plummeted back to being able to tolerate just a handful of seconds alone. We were all stumped, but through considerable cheerleading and after several long talks about the fact that regressions were normal, we were back on track and slowly building up again.

Then came regression number two. Ooof.

Holly began to show us a pattern. She would make progress steadily for a while and then nosedive. Again, and again, and again. Each time she crashed, it was a little less severe than the previous time, and each time we moved forward, it was a bit further than the time before. But it was painstaking and disheartening nonetheless.

One full year into our work together, Deb and Rob decided that they would seek medication counsel. They made an appointment with a renowned veterinary behaviorist, and Holly started on meds. It took many iterations of medication changes and combinations before the right mix was found. More time passed.

After we had a good medication regime and were training for a while, Holly was again chugging along. Then, you guessed it: Holly tumbled hard into another regression. I was devastated, and my confidence was shaken. I could scarcely imagine the disillusionment and frustration that Deb and Rob were feeling about this latest setback.

I made a decision, a hard one. I was not going to be able to help Holly. This was after over a year of working together, so you can imagine how difficult it was going to be to tell Deb and Rob that I no longer had anything to offer them. I felt defeated, and I was questioning absolutely everything that I knew and did with separation anxiety dogs. I'm not gonna lie; it was a miserable time.

I set up an online meeting with Holly's parents to share my decision. Here's what happened on that critically life-altering day.

The online meeting opened up, and there sat Deb and Rob with forlorn faces. I was aching inside at the prospect of telling them the news. Before I had a chance to say anything at all, Deb jumped in and started speaking very seriously.

"Malena, I have an important question for you," she said. "You know that we love Holly with all our hearts and would do absolutely anything for her. We would never give her up, and we would never do anything to compromise her happiness. If we have to, we'll commit to not leaving her alone for the rest of her life."

With a slightly relieved sense, I replied, "I know that, Deb." I was about to continue to speak and explain that a lifetime of management was what I wanted to suggest, but Deb interrupted me.

"Knowing what I just told you, and understanding that Holly is still not better with her separation anxiety, you would never give up on us, right?"

My heart stopped, and my breath caught in my throat. How on earth could I proceed to tell them that I was resigning from their case?

Deb continued, "Since we are committed to never leaving Holly alone, is there any reason that you can see that continuing our training together would not be worth it? I mean, we aren't going to leave her alone anyway, so there's no harm in continuing the gradual process, is there?"

You can imagine how I felt at this instant. For a few moments, I tried to muster up my courage to tell them that we could not proceed, but suddenly I had a flash of clarity. If they were never going to leave Holly alone anyway and the training continued gradually and

Holly

within Holly's threshold, what really was the harm in continuing? Maybe there was a chance that we could eke out further progress over time. In a matter of seconds, I bolted from a place of defeat to a sense of excitement. Maybe I hadn't thought of everything, tried everything. Surely there were things we could try, change, adjust, tweak.

My reply to Deb was simple, and it was certainly not the one I had planned: "Of course, I would never give up on you or Holly."

There it was, all my fears and hopes equally rolled into that one short sentence.

From that day forward, it felt like it was my sole daily purpose to ensure that I helped Holly succeed. I changed very little in our training protocol, but the unyielding conviction that I felt gave me a renewed and focused aim.

But even though Deb and Rob were ready to work indefinitely, that didn't happen. Twelve months after our momentous meeting, Holly had accomplished four hours of calm alone time, and that four hours had been their goal. We were finally victorious, and our time was coming to an end as a result. It was graduation day!

While Deb and Rob were sad to finish their training time with me – after all, we had worked together five days a week for two years – they were undoubtedly delighted to be graduating on such a high note for all of us, especially Holly.

While I fully appreciate that not all clients can devote two years of time, finances, and emotional steadfastness, Holly taught me something that I carry with me to every single client, student, and public seminar. Separation anxiety is fixable.

The experts agree. Voith and Borchelt (1985) note: "If diagnosed and treated correctly, the prognosis for a dog with separation anxiety is excellent." And Sherman and Mills (2008) state that "Owners should be encouraged that it is never too late or a case is never too bad to contemplate treatment, because these factors do not seem to affect prognosis."

And so, I pass on not only the lessons of Holly, but the lessons we have learned from so many more dogs and their wonderful guardians, not to mention the ever-expanding help we get from research.

Malena meets Holly's parents for the first time after working through their separation anxiety protocol.

Conclusion

If you are the guardian of a dog with separation anxiety, I hope this book has helped you understand better what your trainer or behavior consultant is doing. If you are a professional dog trainer or behavior consultant, I hope you can implement the information I've shared here. And if this type of work lights you with excitement and you want to learn more and join a group of like-minded people, you can apply to train as a CSAT yourself.

Working with SA dogs successfully entails thinking both inside and outside the box. Inside the box, we have our carefully planned missions, our spreadsheets, and our data. We teach our clients observation skills and about dog body language. We have these wonderfully data-driven tools that you can use as a guide.

But each dog is an individual. This is why this book doesn't provide a step-by-step process to follow. That's where you are working outside the box. How can we proceed if the dog is stuck at three seconds? How can we better read the particularly subtle signals of this dog approaching threshold? You've probably gotten some ideas for approaching various problems in this book, but solutions will be different for every dog. You will frequently need to come up with creative solutions to unique challenges.

More than anything, we need to have empathy for the dogs and their guardians. Guardians of SA dogs who pursue this training love them dearly. Many have already made enormous changes to their lifestyle to accommodate their dogs' needs. These people need not only our tenderness, but great respect and our best work on behalf of them and their dogs.

The limitations to resolving separation anxiety are bound only by time, and the options to continue to progress through to successful resolution are infinite.

I know the profound difference we can make for separation anxiety dogs with every ounce of my being. I have not only personally worked with so many dogs and guardians but have also watched the successes of so many of the CSATs who have done the same.

As we move forward with technology and use these tools more, we will observe the incredible changes we can make with separation anxiety dogs. My goal is to get this information into the hands of every dog professional that is interested and able to work with separation anxiety so that we can impact the lives of more dogs and those that love them.

The research about separation anxiety has influenced our work tremendously. In closing this book I'd like to thank all those whose incredible contributions to science have allowed us to make this kind of progress in treatment protocols. This quote reminds me that science is ever-evolving and influencing our ability to help animals with various behavior issues:

> *To those with a background in behavior analysis, like ourselves, it is pleasing and historically satisfying to see that systematic desensitization, which grew out of Pavlov's original experimental work using dogs, and then became the treatment of choice for phobias in humans, has proved its worth in increasing the well-being of the very species whose contribution made its development possible." (Butler, 2011)*

If you have taken nothing away from this book other than the belief that separation anxiety is fixable, I feel I have done my job.

References

Appleby, D. & Pluijmakers, J. (2004). Separation anxiety in dogs: The function of homeostasis in its development and treatment. *Clinical Techniques in Small Animal Practice,* 19(4), 205-215.

Ballantyne, K.C. (2018). Separation, Confinement, or Noises: What Is Scaring That Dog? *Veterinary Clinic of North America: Small Animal Practice* 48(3), pp. 367-386.

Blackwell, E., Casey, R.A. & Bradshaw, J.W.S. (2006). Controlled trial of behavioural therapy for separation-related disorders in dogs. *Veterinary Record* 158(16), 551-554. doi: 10.1136/vr.158.16.551.

Bonn-Miller, M.O. et al. (2017). Labeling Accuracy of Cannabidiol Extracts Sold Online. *JAMA,* 318(17):1708-1709.

Borchelt, P.L. & Voith, V.L. (1982). Diagnosis and Treatment of Separation-Related Behavior Problems in Dogs. *Symposium on Animal Behavior,* 625-635.

Bradshaw, J.W.S., et al. (2002). Aetiology of separation-related behaviour in domestic dogs. *The Veterinary Record* 151(2), 43-46. doi: 10.1136/vr.151.2.43.

Brady, H. (2017): This is your brain on puppy pictures. *National Geographic,* March 23, 2017: https://www.nationalgeographic.com/news/2017/03/national-puppy-day-vintage-pictures/.

Butler, R., Sargisson, R. J. & Elliffe, D. (2011). The efficacy of systematic desensitization for treating the separation-related problem behaviour of domestic dogs. *Applied Animal Behaviour Science,* 129(2), 136-145.

Cannas, S. et al. (2010). Puppy behavior when left home alone: Changes during the first few months after adoption. *Journal of Veterinary Behavior: Clinical Applications and Research* 5, 94–100.

Cannas, S., et al. (2014). Video analysis of dogs suffering from anxiety when left home alone and treated with clomipramine. *Journal of Veterinary Behavior: Clinical Applications and Research* 9, 50–57.

Cottam, N., et al. (2008). Comparison of Remote Versus In-Person Behavioral Consultation for Treatment of Canine Separation Anxiety, *Journal of Applied Animal Welfare Science* 11:1, 28-41.

de Assis, L.S. et al. (2020). Developing Diagnostic Frameworks in Veterinary Behavioral Medicine: Disambiguating Separation Related Problems in Dogs. *Frontiers in Veterinary Science* 6(499).

FDA: What You Need to Know (And What We're Working to Find Out) About Products Containing Cannabis or Cannabis-derived Compounds, Including CBD. Available at https://www.fda.gov/consumers/consumer-updates/what-you-need-know-and-what-were-working-find-out-about-products-containing-cannabis-or-cannabis.

Feuerbacher, E. & Muir, K. (2020). Using Owner Return as a Reinforcer to Operantly Treat Separation-Related Problem Behavior in Dogs. Animals 10(7), 1-20.

Flannigan, G. & Dodman, N.H. (2001). Risk factors and behaviors associated with separation anxiety in dogs. *Journal of the American Veterinary Medical Association* 219(4), 460-466.

Green (2014). Loyalty Gone Overboard, Separation Anxiety: "The Velcro Dog Dilemma". Good News for Pets: http://goodnewsforpets.com/loyalty-gone-overboard-separation-anxiety-velcro-dog-dilemma/.

Herron, M.E., Lord, L.K., Husseini, S.E. (2014). Effects of preadoption counseling on the prevention of separation anxiety in newly adopted shelter dogs. *Journal of Veterinary Behavior: Clinical Applications and Research* 9, 13–21.

Hetts, S. (2012). The Latest on Separation Anxiety. *Integrative Veterinary Care Journal.*

Lopes Fagundes, A.L. et al. (2018). Noise Sensitivities in Dogs: An Exploration of Signs in Dogs with and without Musculoskeletal Pain Using Qualitative Content Analysis. *Front. Vet. Sci.* 5(17).

Lund, J.D. & Jørgensen, M.C. (1999). Behaviour patterns and time course of activity in dogs with separation problems. *Applied Animal Behaviour Science* 63(3), 219-236.

Mariti et al. (2012). Perception of dogs' stress by their owners. *Journal of Veterinary Behavior* 7(4), 213-219.

McCrave, E.A., Lung N. & Voith, V.L. (1986). Correlates of separation anxiety in the dog. In *Abstracts of the Delta Society International Conference,* Boston, p. 124.

McCrave, E.A. (1991). Diagnostic criteria for separation anxiety in the dog. *Veterinary Clinics of North America: Small Animal Practice* 21(2), 247-255.

McKenzie, B. (2020). Do pulsed electromagnetic field devices offer any benefit? *Veterinary Practice News:* https://www.veterinarypracticenews.com/pemf-january-2020/.

Mervis, C.B. et al. (2012). Duplication of GTF21 Results in Separation Anxiety in Mice and Humans. *The American Journal of Human Genetics* 90, 1064–1070.

Miranda, C. (2018). How to Market CBD Products in the Sea of Uncertainty. Cannabis Business Executive: https://www.cannabisbusinessexecutive.com/2018/08/market-cbd-products-sea-uncertainty/.

O'Farrell, V. (1986). *Manual of Canine Behaviour.* British Small Animal Veterinary Assoc, Cheltenham.

Ogata, N. & Dodman, N. (2011). The use of clonidine in the treatment of fear-based behavior problems in dogs: An open trial. *Journal of Veterinary Behavior* 6(2) 130-137.

Ogata, N. (2016) Separation anxiety in dogs: What progress has been made in our understanding of the most common behavioral problems in dogs? *Journal of Veterinary Behavior Clinical Applications and Research* 16, 28-35.

Parthasarathy, V. & Crowell-Davis, S.L. (2006). Relationship between attachment to owners and separation anxiety in pet dogs (Canis lupus familiaris). *Journal of Veterinary Behavior: Clinical Applications and Research* 1(3), 109-120.

Rooy, D. et al. (2016). Evaluating candidate genes oprm1, drd2, avpr1a, and oxtr in golden retrievers with separation-related behaviors. *Journal of Veterinary Behavior* 16:22-27.

Sargisson, R. (2014). Canine separation anxiety: strategies for treatment and management. *Veterinary Medicine: Research and Reports* 143.

Sherman, B.L. & Mills, D.S. (2008). Canine anxieties and phobias: an update on separation anxiety and noise aversions. *Veterinary Clinics of North America: Small Animal Practice* 38(5), 1081-1106.

Sinn, L. (2018). Advances in Behavioral Psychopharmacology. *Vet Clin Small Anim* 48:457-471

Tiira, K., Sulkama, S. & Lohi, H. (2016). Prevalence, comorbidity, and behavioral variation in canine anxiety. *Journal of Veterinary Behavior* 16, 36–44.

Tschorn, A (2017). "Don't Try to Treat Your Pet's Anxiety With Pot – Until You Read This." LA Times: https://www.latimes.com/style/pets/la-hm-pets-cannabis-for-your-pet-20170827-story.html.

Turner, D.C. (1997). Treating canine and feline behaviour problems and advising clients. *Applied Animal Behaviour Science* 52, 199–204.

Voith, V.L. & Borchelt, P.L. (1985). Separation anxiety in dogs. *Compend Contin Educ Pract Vet* 7:42-53.

Voith, V.L., Wright, J.C. & Danneman, P.J. (1992). Is there a relationship between canine behavior problems and spoiling activities, anthropomorphism, and obedience training? *Applied Animal Behaviour Science* 34, 263–272.

Wright, J.C. & Nesselrote, M.S. (1987). Classification of behavior problems in dogs: Distributions of age, breed, sex and reproductive status. *Applied Animal Behaviour Science* 19, 169–178.

Resources and
Additional Reading

Amat, M. et al. (2014). Separation anxiety in dogs: the implications of predictability and contextual fear for behavioural treatment. *Animal Welfare* 23:263-266.

Ashe, C. (2019). Know Your CBDs. *Whole Dog Journal:* https://www.whole-dog-journal.com/care/know-your-cbds/

Blackwell, E., Bradshaw, J.W.S. & Casey, R.A. (2013). Fear responses to noises in domestic dogs: Prevalence, risk factors and co-occurrence with other fear related behaviour. *Applied Animal Behaviour Science* 145(1), 15-25.

Buckley, L.A. (2018). Are Pressure Vests Beneficial at Reducing Stress in Anxious and Fearful Dogs? *Veterinary Evidence* 3(1) 1-21.

Canine Companion Consulting, email newsletter: https://mailchi.mp/97252a50a29f/cbd-dogs-what-do-we-know

Dr. Jens Blog

Fox, M.W. (1968). *Abnormal Behavior in Animals.* Philadelphia: Saunders.

Kovács, K. et al. (2018). Dog-Owner Attachment Is Associated With Oxytocin Receptor Gene Polymorphisms in Both Parties. A Comparative Study on Austrian and Hungarian Border Collies. *Front. Psychol.* 9:435.

Mariti, C., et al. (2012). Perception of dogs' stress by their owners. *Journal of Veterinary Behavior: Clinical Applications and Research* 7(4), 213-219.

McGreevy, P.D. & Masters, A.M. (2008). Risk factors for separation-related distress and feed-related aggression in dogs: additional findings from a survey of Australian dog owners. *Applied Animal Behaviour Science* 109(2), 320-328.

Overall, K.L. (2013). *Manual of Clinical Behavioral Medicine for Dogs and Cats.* Mosby.

Overall, K.L., Dunham, A.E. & Frank, D. (2001). Frequency of nonspecific clinical signs in dogs with separation anxiety, thunderstorm phobia, and noise phobia, alone or in combination. *Journal of the American Veterinary Medical Association* 219(4), 467-473.

Palestrini, C., et al. (2010). Video analysis of dogs with separation-related behaviors. *Applied Animal Behaviour Science* 124(1), 61-67. doi: 10.1016/j.applanim.2010.01.014.

Payne, E., Bennett, P.C. & McGreevy, P.D. (2015). Current perspectives on attachment and bonding in the dog-human dyad. *Psychol Res Behav Manag.* 8:71–79, doi:10.2147/PRBM.S74972.

Rehn, T. & Keeling, L.J. (2011). The effect of time left alone at home on dog welfare. *Applied Animal Behaviour Science* 129, 129–135.

Scaglia, E., et al. (2013). Video analysis of adult dogs when left home alone. *Journal of Veterinary Behavior: Clinical Applications and Research* 8, 412–417.

Simpson, B.S., et al. (2007). Effects of reconcile (fluoxetine) chewable tablets plus behavior management for canine separation anxiety. *Veterinary Therapeutics* 8(1):18-31.

Sinn, L. (2018). Advances in Behavioral Psychopharmacology. *Vet Clin Small Anim* 48:457-471.

Takeuchi, Y., et al. (2001). Differences in background and outcome of three behavior problems of dogs. *Applied Animal Behaviour Science* 70, 297–308.

Todd, Z. (2018). Barriers to the adoption of humane dog training methods. *Journal of Veterinary Behavior* 25, 28–34.

Zapata et al. (2016). Genetic mapping of canine fear and aggression. *BMC Genomics* 17:572.

About the Author

Malena DeMartini-Price is renowned in the dog training world for her expertise in canine separation anxiety. She has contributed articles about separation anxiety to multiple publications around the world including professional trade magazines as well as national magazines both in and out of the dog industry. She lectures on separation anxiety at professional dog training workshops and conferences worldwide, including everything from large professional conferences to small venues. She also has been interviewed widely on this topic and multiple videos and podcasts have been produced. Malena is an honors graduate of the esteemed Academy for Dog Trainers, where she studied under Jean Donaldson, and is a member of the APDT, the PPG and the IAABC.

Malena has focused exclusively on SA since 2001, working many hundreds of cases and constantly innovating to find better ways to work with the condition and support clients.

Today, her practice is split between overseeing a team of top SA trainers in the world and continuing to educate trainers, veterinarians and dog guardians to better treat separation anxiety, in order to help the greatest number of dogs and humans possible to overcome this agonizing issue. In addition to writing and lecturing, Malena runs a certification program for accomplished dog professionals looking to hone their skills and has also produced an online self-paced course for dog owners.

Malena lives in Northern California with her husband – also a certified dog trainer – and their dog, Tini DeMartini, who is a recovered separation anxiety dog.

Index

Also available from Dogwise Publishing

Go to www.dogwise.com for more books and ebooks.

The Human Half of Dog Training

COLLABORATING WITH CLIENTS TO GET RESULTS

Risë VanFleet, PhD, CDBC

Dog trainers don't really train dogs—they train people to train their dogs. Learn how to empathize with clients, overcome common objections and work with families to get the best results for the dog. From a PhD Psychologist-turned-dog-trainer.

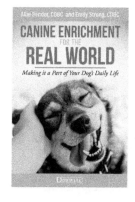

Canine Enrichment for the Real World

MAKING IT A PART OF YOUR DOG'S DAILY LIFE

Allie Bender, CDBC and Emily Strong, CDBC

In the world of dogs, there is more awareness of the need to provide enrichment activities, especially in shelters. Authors Strong and Bender provide you with real world ideas to help you enrich your dog's everyday life.

On Talking Terms with Dogs

CALMING SIGNALS, 2ND ED.

Turid Rugaas

Norwegian dog trainer and behaviorist Turid Rugaas has made it her life work to study canine social interaction. Yawning, lip-licking, sneezing, even scratching are just a few of the 30-plus signals that dogs use to communicate with one another.

Canine Body Language

A PHOTOGRAPHIC GUIDE

Brenda Aloff

Your dog is "talking." Are you listening? Dogs are attempting to communicate with humans as well as other dogs all the time. It's up to us to learn how to interpret their native language—the language of body movement, facial expression and proximity to things and other beings.

Lightning Source UK Ltd.
Milton Keynes UK
UKHW021234190721
387406UK00010B/2132